Th[...]

f[...] you[...]

[...]

Chris[...]

The Joy is in
the Suffering

The Joy is in the Suffering

C H R I S T I N A   R I E D L E   F R Y E

TATE PUBLISHING
AND ENTERPRISES, LLC

Published by Tate Publishing & Enterprises, LLC
127 E. Trade Center Terrace | Mustang, Oklahoma 73064 USA
1.888.361.9473 | www.tatepublishing.com

Tate Publishing is committed to excellence in the publishing industry. The company reflects the philosophy established by the founders, based on Psalm 68:11,
"The Lord gave the word and great was the company of those who published it."

Book design copyright © 2012 by Tate Publishing, LLC. All rights reserved.
Cover design by Rodrigo Adolfo
Interior design by Ronnel Luspoc

Published in the United States of America

ISBN: 978-1-62295-450-6
1. Biography & Autobiography / Personal Memoirs
2. Religion / Christian Life / Death, Grief, Bereavement
12.12.18

Dedication

This was written in honor of the life and death of my brother Joshua Matthew. He will never see the mark his death has left on our family and so many other individuals and their families. Through his death so many, including his family, walk a little closer with thee. Josh was a great man that led his family to Christ and left a legacy for his child and grandchildren to come, and now those that will read this manuscript.

Most importantly, this is dedicated to Christ. Without His continued whisperings to my soul to write, this would have never been written. I have been truly humbled to be the vessel. I now realize that the sewn frayed ends of the quilt are so much more beautiful from the top, even though I haven't seen it yet. God bless, as we all wait for the glorious day.

Acknowledgments

My heartfelt thanks to the support of my church, Holy Cross, and the anonymous individuals that helped make this happen.

To Pastor Wade, without you, your guidance, instruction and support, I would have never come through this whole and changed. I am truly blessed to call you friend and minister. From the bottom of my heart, I thank you.

To Pastor Ryan, for being with this suffering family, from church that fateful day and then the hospital, through the funeral and on. Thanks for reading this and blessing it.

To Pastor Sutton, for reading this manuscript and being honest with your thoughts and understanding our suffering through these words.

Thanks to Matt, one of the first responders, for being with him, for helping him, and for never forgetting him or this family. The bracelet you wear is a constant reminder of that day.

Thanks to all the medical staff, from the first responders to the doctors and nurses. Thank you for doing your best while making Josh comfortable.

To my parents, that without their godly instruction my whole life, this book wouldn't have been possible. They laid the foundation for me as a young child to continue as an adult while leaving my own legacy for my children. To my mother especially, who knew early on I was writing this. Thanks for always reading it and telling me how beautiful it was. Also, for never doubting that it would make it to publication, for others to read its beauty.

To my friend Amy, who has stood by me since December 21, 2008. Thank you for always listening, crying and laughing with me. Thanks for encouraging me to continue writing and never doubting why I was doing this. Thanks for hearing and believing in the "yapping."

To my children, the lights of my life, who inspire me every day to leave them a legacy worth telling people about.

Thanks to my husband for stepping in to help my parents when they needed it the most and sticking by them. Also, for all the love and support he has given us all since December 21, 2008.

To all my family and friends, thanks for the continued prayers and support.

Preface

December 21, 2008 was a life-changing event that moved our lives forever. We lost a valuable member of our family after two days in the local ICU. His life not only saved others' lives, as he was an organ donor, but his death has changed his families' lives and others. After a long period of suffering, God started to tug on my soul to write, by starting with Josh's death. Death changes the people left to mourn, not only those that have died. They are taken home to dance with the saints while we are left to suffer. This was born out of suffering and joy. This suffering has transformed my life and the idea of salvation. There is a destination after this earthly realm we are living in and the way we live it today may indicate were we spend it tomorrow. Eternal salvation is what the goal is and should be for all. I have learned that I plan to run this race till the end, to be united with God and reunited with Josh. This work is about one sister's quest for eternal life, and how important it is to get the world on board with that idea.

The Lord Has Done It

It started out like no other day and ended in a nightmare. You never know when a day or moment will change your life forever and your perspective on life. It was Sunday, December 21, 2008, and we were getting ready to celebrate the life of a five-year-old boy. We were having a birthday party for our son, Jacob, and it was the coldest, windiest day in December thus far. We were experiencing some difficulties with our furnace, and as we rose out of bed, it was not only bitterly cold outside, but inside as well. The thermostat was set on seventy-two, and it was fifty-two in the house, and we had a party to get ready for. As I was rushing around in a panic, trying to get up and ready, my husband was trying to fix the furnace for the umpteenth time. Once again, he did manage to rig the furnace, however, we knew it is only a matter of time before the flame blew out again. As everyone was busy getting ready, and my husband was patting himself on the back for being a good handyman, I could see nothing but disaster for a five-year-old and his party.

Family started to arrive and come into the cold house. The first guests to arrive were my brother Josh and his family. As I was pulling them in quickly, to conserve heat, it dawned on me that my brother hadn't seen the Christmas gift we'd bought together for our father. There are three of us children, and we usually try to go in together on gifts for our parents, and this year was a good one. I couldn't wait for Dad to open it in a couple days, on Christmas day. Josh came into the bedroom as I took out this wooden-framed, hand-painted picture of our father's grandparents' old homestead. The painting was an aerial shot that was then hand-painted on canvas. Oh boy, Dad was going to love it, especially because the homestead no longer stands on the farmland. Josh loved it and said Dad would too. He rushed Betsy, his wife, in to see it before my dad made it in the house.

Soon, everyone else had arrived for Jacob's birthday, and no one really complained about the icicles growing off their noses. I did throw some blankets on Josh and Betsy just in case. As a family, we did all the normal birthday stuff; I caught Josh grabbing Jacob and swatting him on the butt for five counts and giving him one to grow on. We all visited; we sang happy birthday; and my sister, brother, and I added in "you smell like a monkey and you look like one to" and a "do-do-do" after each line—you know, the little family traditions throughout the years that stick. Jacob then blew out the candles, opened his gifts, and that was pretty much it. Nothing disastrous here; we escaped unscathed. My brother was trying to make arrangements with all of us to come over and help with inventory at the shop during New Year's. Normal, everyday, run of the mill, family kinds of things. We said our good-byes.

My brother and his family headed home. Soon after, my parents, sister and her family left to attend my niece's Christmas program at their church. After they were all gone, I proceeded to clean up, and my husband continued to tend to the furnace. On Sunday, HVAC guys don't work, but my husband's furnace guy would be there bright and early Monday to fix it. I got the vacuum out and started running it, and I could see my cell phone lighting up. I have missed my dad's call.

I thought, *Oh well, I will finish the vacuuming and call him back.*

I listened to a message my dad didn't intend to leave, and I could hear that his voice was a little panicky. He said, "She didn't answer." He is talking to my mother. I called back hurriedly. Finally, my mother answered and said, "Josh, Betsy, and Olivia have been in a car accident, and all Betsy can tell me is: 'he is breathing.'"

Now, I clearly understood the panic in my father's voice. I'd like to think, and tell people, that I am pretty good in a crisis—after all, I am a therapist and deal with crisis a lot. Truth is, I am horrible in a crisis, and I go into complete meltdown and panic mode very quickly. If panic were rated on a speedometer, I would be at one hundred ten in no time flat.

I told my mother that I would be at the local hospital as soon as I could; it was thirty miles away, and I had to find a place for my kids to go. She told me not to call Betsy; she was dealing with the police, ambulance, and the current situation.

Lucky for me, my husband's sister and kids were home for the holidays, and she said she would watch our children. Angella and I were great friends even before I married her brother. I met my husband because I was a friend of hers. Needless to say, she was also a friend of my brother Josh and my family, so she was more than willing to take care of our children so we could head to the hospital. We drove to my in-laws. Angella met me outside, hugged me, told me she loved me, and then, we were on our way to the hospital. On our drive, my husband, also Josh, was telling me things like: "It is probably just a concussion, he will be in and out of the hospital, and he will be fine." In fact, he was so certain it was "nothing" that, originally, he was going to stay home with the children. I tend to be more pes-simistic than my husband, and as I was continuing to lose it, he was telling me to calm down. In my gut, I felt that something was terribly wrong. Most of the time, my gut is correct. He didn't understand why I was in panic mode, but when I'd heard from my mother, "All I can tell you is that he is breathing," I went into panic mode. We had already experienced tragedy one and a half years earlier when we lost our oldest brother to an overdose, so yes, I panicked.

The thirty-mile drive in bone-chilling cold wind seemed to take hours. I was in contact with my mother throughout the drive, but Sara, my identical twin sister, had decided to stay at her children's Christmas program and come to the hospital afterwards; she was under the same notion as my husband. As we were just about to pass her church, I got a call from my mother, telling me to stop and pick Sara up because, she said, "Josh isn't going to make it." The words were out. The big pur-ple elephant that I'd felt was standing in the room was finally exposed. My heart sank, and I looked at my hus-band. Without saying a word, he knew. I suddenly felt like we were in the Indy 500, taking the corner on two wheels as he sped to the church. I jumped out, trying to figure out which door to go into so as not to completely disrupt the service.

Her church is much like every big, old Lutheran church; it had many entrances and was filled with people watching their children and grandchildren perform at the Christmas program. I stood in the front, almost next to the pulpit, and no one noticed. Sara and her husband weren't answering my text messages, and I couldn't see her through the vast amounts of people. It was like I was a lost child looking for my mother or someone I knew in a crowd. I just needed to recognize a face and run to them for safety. I was looking into a sea of unfamiliar faces, and was not able to connect with any of them. It seemed as if no one was paying any attention to the distressed woman. They were watching the little children in the Christmas program, and I was just somebody looking for a seat in the packed pews. Finally a woman, who I knew saw the dread on my face, came to help me.

Sara and I are identical twins. When I told her who I needed, she said, "She looks a lot like you. I have seen her; I will go get her."

I could see the woman make her way through the droves of Christians that filled the church until she found Sara and her family. Here, Sara came with her youngest child, Mariah, soon to be three, on her hip as I was grasping for the words to say, "Josh is dying." I explained the direness of what Mom had just told me on the phone. She understood by looking at my face, twin intuition or just pure fear on my face, one will never know.

The hospital was only five miles away, but it felt like forever. This is the hospital that all my children were born in. Joyful memories of this place were being replaced with painful ones. As we drove the rest of the way, we held each other's hands, me in the front seat, Sara in the back. I kept yelling, "This can't be happening!" I wanted to look at my husband and say, "Now can I panic?"

My husband dropped us off at ER, and he parked the car. Everyone was there, waiting. They were getting ready to wheel Josh out to the helicopter on the gurney as we arrived. The EMT, Matt, that was called to the accident sight was still with him. He happened to look up at Sara, and they fixed their eyes on each other. They recognized one another as parents from the same Lutheran school that their children go to. His face grimaced as he realized that he now knew this family, our family. My father looked up and thanked Matt for what he had done to help his son. Matt would later tell my sister that he couldn't believe that my father had thanked *him* that night, seeing that we were in the middle of distress.

When I got to see Josh, his eyes were closed, he was lifeless, just breathing. A hospital gurney is never a good look for anyone with tubes, a neck brace, and blood pressure cup, all the normal medical equipment. This was not how he'd looked hours ago upon leaving my house. He was full of life and ambition. *This isn't the same man, right?* I looked up and saw red particles on Betsy's sweater, and I suddenly knew what these red particles were and what the depth of his head injury was without asking. For a brief second, I thought about brushing the flakes off, but I'm thankful didn't.

The medical staff handed my mother a bag of Josh's belongings that they took off of him. I fell to pieces as they handed her this bag of belongings. These were the things that he was just wearing; these things that were probably still warm from his body, the bag of things that belonged to Josh. It was as if the US Army was handing her a folded up flag in honor of a fallen solider.

As I watched this unfold, I thought, *How can this be possible? This is a man that was sitting on my couch less than two hours ago, alive and well, planning a weekend of inventory over New Years for the business he owned with my father. It is not possible that our family is suffering this way, after celebrating a five-year-old's birth, and so close to Christmas. This isn't possible...*

Only God Can Count the Number of Apples in a Seed

If you have read Matthew 26:39 (NIV), then you know anything is possible: "Going a little farther, he fell with his face to the ground and prayed, 'My Father, if it is possible, may this cup be taken from me. Yet not as I will, but as you will.'" It was possible that God the Father was going to allow His Son to bear the cross that the human race burdened to Him. This was Jesus's fate even before he was born, but Jesus knew that too. If God could let his own son be nailed to a cross for me, it was completely possible that He would allow us to be in our nightmare. See Jesus's days were numbered just as ours are. Much as I was doing, Jesus continued praying to our Father that He would release him from this destiny: Mark 14:35 (NIV), "Going a little farther, he fell to the ground and prayed that if possible the hour might pass from him." Again, our Father remained still. You see, the possibilities in this world are endless, like the number of apples in a seed, and it is only the arrogance of human nature that tells us: *This can't be happening to us.* It is said in Isaiah 45:

> I am the LORD, and there is no other; apart from me there is no God. I will strengthen you, though you have not acknowledged me, so that from the rising of the sun to the place of its set-

ting people may know there is none besides me.
I am the LORD, and there is no other. I form the
light and create darkness, I bring prosperity and
create disaster; I, the LORD, do all these things.

Isaiah 45:5-7 (NIV)

I guess this was happening, and it was happening
because the Lord was allowing it. Reality is these things
are never impossible. We also discovered he follows
through with His word. While this was happening, we
were given the strength to endure what was ahead and
we were to be delivered from all evils:

But the Lord stood at my side and gave me
strength, so that through me the message might
be fully proclaimed and all the Gentiles might
hear it. And I was delivered from the lion's
mouth. The Lord will rescue me from every evil
attack and will bring me safely to his heavenly
kingdom. To him be glory for ever and ever.
Amen.

2 Timothy 4:17-18 (NIV)

Isn't there always a message or purpose in God's
works? We all know the message from the death of
Christ. I am sure there is a purpose for this suffering
and a message to be proclaimed.

At this point, we were all still immobilized with
shock and fear. It still seemed utterly impossible that
our family was enduring this tragedy. This couldn't be
happening. This wasn't happening. This was impossible.
Why was this happening? But the implausible situation was happening. The impossible continued to hap-

pen. It was impossible that they were loading him into the helicopter to fly him to the local trauma center, another forty-five-minute drive north for us, and in Oz-like winds. It was impossible that we might not get to see him alive again; it was impossible that God would allow tragedy to once again rear its ugly head in our family, so you can understand how it was impossible that our family might have to experience this again. Paralyzed, I started to ask questions. Is this a double whammy? What did we do? Wasn't losing our eldest brother enough? The answer was no. The first loss wasn't enough and it was completely possible, again. This heavy burden we were bearing was very real, and reality is, if Christ can go to the cross, the Father's only son, then why can't we? Christ's burden was heavier than ours ever will be.

We watched the medical staff roll him out to the helicopter, and we hurriedly said good-bye to Olivia and got into our vehicles. The drive north in the cold headwind was treacherous; it never gave us a break. Illinois is known for crazy weather, and Mother Nature was unrelenting that night. If we had only known how cold it was really going to get. How can you be in a car full of people but still feel so alone? I was lost in the moment, confused and disoriented, and I felt like the only person in the world who was suffering, and yet my whole family was suffering along with me. However, suffering is very personal and selfish. There is something about fear and suffering that keeps you locked inside of self-pity, and if you can't get to God, you will be trapped. "You needed to snap out of it," as my pastor would say. Remember Romans 8:18 (NIV): "I consider that our present sufferings are not worth comparing with the glory that will be revealed in us." We were far from understanding the glory aspect of it all.

Over the next forty-five minutes, I tried to focus, wrap my mind around the impossible and digest what was truly happening and what we needed to do as a family. I called everyone I could think of that needed to know. I called my minister first to start the prayer chain and inform him of the situation. I then called my boss to apprise her of the events and inform her that I might not be to work for a while. I know that my family in this caravan north were all thinking and feeling the same things and were, of course, hoping for a healing miracle in between the moments of total shell shock from this war and disbelief. Yet we didn't know we were at war. The enemy ambushed us, caught us off guard, and our only counterattack was Christ.

First Thessalonians 5:16-18 (NIV) says, "Rejoice always, pray continually, give thanks in all circumstances; for this is God's will for you in Christ Jesus." For anyone that has been in a similar situation or in any real discomfort, you know that the first part of that verse isn't as difficult as the last part, especially after an ambush like this. How many of us give praise and glory to God when we are at war? There was a purpose for this, but to give thanks in all circumstances is tough when you aren't sure whether your brother is alive or dead. However, this is one thing that is required of us. Your mind and heart tell you to pray that God spares his life and that we all go on living like we were but that we will learn and grow from the circumstance. Yet God is telling us we should be praying, and we should be giving thanks for the circumstance at hand, the thunderstorm pelting us with golf-ball-sized hail in a F5 tornado. I am pretty sure none of us gave thanks for the hail or the tornado. I guess that makes me a sinful human being, like everyone. It comes down to faith. Faith like a mustard seed. Faith that God's will will be done, whatever that is for any particular situation. Faith believes that God has a plan that we just don't see or understand yet and may never. However, we trust that it exists for a purpose. We trust in His grace and mercy. "Trust in the Lord with all your heart and lean not on your own understanding" (Proverbs 3:5, NIV). When you lean unto your own understanding, we misinterpret things, and thoughts, words, and actions become skewed. That's when sin can set in.

In retrospect, I am astonished and a little ashamed of the pompous thoughts that invaded my mind in this great moment of distress. One of the most intrusive and arrogant thoughts was, *God couldn't and wouldn't do this again to us; after all, he has already taken home my eldest brother, he won't take another.* How arrogant and sinful of me to even ponder that thought. It was just another way of my mind trying to convince my heart that this was impossible. Yet being a follower of Christ, I know that tragic things are allowed to happen all the time. It doesn't matter who you are or how much you have endured already in our life. I am reminded of a popular Christian song called *Blessings* by Laura Story, maybe these are our mercies in disguise.

Do you think Job believed his sufferings were mercies from God, the whole time he suffered?

I learned about Job and his sufferings, how God allowed Satan to test him but not to touch a hair on Job's head. God allowed Satan to bring him to trials and tribulations. In Job 1:12 (NIV), the Lord said to Satan, "Very well, then, everything he has is in your power, but on the man himself do not lay a finger." This is God saying, "I will let you distress my servant Job." As a result, Job suffered much pain, distress, anguish, and grief, but he remained faithful. Satan couldn't shatter his faithfulness or his trust in God. I knew, no matter what, I must be like Job and remain faithful to the Lord through this. I must lead my children through this faithfully. God is our fortress and strength. "But I will sing of your strength, in the morning I will sing of your love; for you are my fortress, my refuge in times of trouble." (Psalms 59:16, NIV), and again, in Philippians 4:13: "I can do all this through him who gives me strength." This last verse has to be one of the most uplifting verses in the Bible. God is telling us right there that all we need is him to get through it all. To get through this earthly realm and to get through our grief, mourning, pain and distress. Job believed it. Why don't we? The words of Romans 12:12(NIV) came to mind; "Be joyful in hope, patient in affliction, faithful in prayer." Like our friend Job.

There did come a day that the trials and tribulations ended for Job. I like to think of it as one of the days Satan lost. Afterward, as a reward for his faithfulness God blessed Job. "The Lord blessed the latter part of Job's life more than the former part." (Job 42:1-2 NIV),

All for his faithfulness. This was a man that was loved and protected by God, even though God allowed Satan to test him. I guess it is possible that God will allow this tragedy to happen, and it is up to us whether we stay faithful and reap the blessings, like Job, or we turn away and suffer more losses. I am not well versed on how you measure blessings or how you know if you are more blessed now than you were before, but God said Job was. What I do understand is this, Job had God's grace and mercy bestowed upon him.

After re-reading the book of Job, I have to admit, that Job and I aren't even in the same ballpark in terms of loss and distress, but it is all-relevant, isn't it? Job had some curve balls thrown at him and so have I, so have most. It is not about how many curve balls have been sent your way; it's about how many times you stepped into the batters box and kept swinging. God doesn't want his people to give up, he wants them to keep fighting and trust in him. 2 Timothy 4:7(NIV) shows us this "I have fought the good fight, I have finished the race, I have kept the faith." Despite the devastation that comes with any tragic moment in our lives, God doesn't want us to turn away and be with our own devices. God wants us to come to him and trust in him, God wants us to need him. He wants us to keep swinging and stay in the game. He wants us to keep running the race, and we do this by falling to our knees and praying faithfully. This is how we keep swinging, by continuing to pray fervently and continuously. My parents minister, Pastor Sutton pointed out to me once, that prayer is a means of grace and a way of communicating back and forth with our Father.

This could be a private or public display such as church or prayers groups. Prayer ultimately comforts us and assures us of our forgiveness in Christ. Just another way that God preaches His gospel into our hearts. However, at the time, faithful and fervent prayers were not coming to my mind like I would have thought or hoped. After all, in my world of impossibilities, this is the time I should be on my knees, but the words weren't flowing. Even the thoughts didn't make a lot of sense because they were jumbled and my mind was running faster than anything else, although, the thoughts are always there. Think about it, ha, you were already thinking about it. And when you think you weren't thinking, you were thinking about not thinking. It's an endless cycle and sometimes the things that go through your mind or the words that come out of your mouth in situations of great distress and fear aren't always rational. I am sure I sounded like a complete buffoon sometimes, unlike Job and his prayers, and other times, I couldn't even formulate thoughts or sentences, let alone prayers. When I wanted to pray, I couldn't find the words. Romans 8 is very clear about these moments when you can't formulate the words:

> In the same way, the Spirit helps us in our weakness. We do not know what we ought to pray for, but the Spirit himself intercedes for us through wordless groans. And he who searches our hearts knows the mind of the Spirit, because the Spirit intercedes for God's people in accordance with the will of God.
>
> Romans 8:26-27 (NIV)

The Spirit knew through my groans what I needed; words weren't needed. Hebrew 7:25 (NIV) also addresses intercession, but from Jesus himself, on our behalf: "Therefore he is able to save completely those who come to God through him, because he always lives to intercede for them." *Always.*

Some of you might be thinking that it should be easy in crisis to immediately turn to God and pray, or that I must not know who Christ really is or what God can do for me. Let me explain: It isn't as if I didn't have a relationship with God or know that I am a sinner that is forgiven and saved by grace. It wasn't that I didn't know how to pray or even that it was awkward because I am not spiritual. You see, I come from a pretty long line of devout Missouri Synod Lutherans. As a matter of fact, this was Sunday, and before driving to the party my parents, Josh, Betsy, and their daughter Olivia had been in church together. I know about God, what the Bible teaches me, but there are moments in life that stop you in your tracks and you forget, even if only for a split second, which way is up, while you are walking in a circle. I know that my parents feel blessed that they spent the morning in church receiving the body and the blood of Jesus Christ in Holy Communion, with their son and praying. In the adult Bible class that day, the question was asked, that became oh so real for them just hours after hearing it: "Why does God take the young?" Pastor Ryan had a classic response: "We don't know, but God is always just and right. He is never wrong." God was preparing them and they didn't even know it. That is one of the wonderful things about God, as I say in retrospect: he prepares you even when you aren't aware. I believe that the Spirit was already intervening on their behalf during the church service and adult Bible class because soon we would know we need that intercession, just not quite yet. Really, when you look at it, wasn't this a blessing in disguise for my parents? I mean, doesn't it seem as if God blessed them by allowing them to spend this morning together, loving and worshiping God? Wasn't God already preparing them in the adult Bible class by listening to pastor talk about the loss of young people? My opinion is yes. Yes, the whole day was a blessing for us because some never see their loved ones before or after a tragic accident. Some never sit together in church and receive the body and blood of Christ before being separated, and some never get to say good-bye. We did. God was telling them, even in Bible class that day, *It is not impossible.*

"The riddles of God are more
satisfying than the solutions
of man." (G.K. Chesterton)

Driving into the unknown is grueling. We knew where we were going, but not knowing what was ahead for Josh's life was painful and excruciating. For all we knew, he had awakened in the life flight helicopter and was joking and being his normal self, or he could have been escorted home already, and we didn't get to say good-bye. The not knowing is very difficult in any circumstance, not just ours. God is the only one that knows the day time and place, not even His son. I wonder if Jesus ever wondered if His Father would intervene on his behalf and save him from the cross. I wonder if Christ ever felt similar to this hoping for his Fathers return before he went to the cross. But of course Christ new this was his destiny. Matthew 24:36 (NIV) "But about that day or hour no one knows, not even the angels in heaven, nor the Son, but only the Father." Everyone understands the unknown return of Christ, right? No one other than God himself knows the hour and the day when we will be separated into sheep and goats. It is written in the New Testament, from Matthew 25:

> When the Son of Man comes in his glory, and all the angels with him, he will sit on his glorious throne. All the nations will be gathered

before him, and he will separate the people one from another as a shepherd separates the sheep from the goats. He will put the sheep on his right and the goats on his left.

Matthew 25:31-33 (NIV)

Funny how this unknown isn't something most church-going, God-fearing sinners, think about, worry about, or concern ourselves with until life-changing events occur. In all honesty, we get up and go about our day without a thought of the unknown day in front of us. We hear the buzz of the alarm clock in the mornings, and we don't think about or wonder if this is the day that Michael and Gabriel will come with their trumpets. "Therefore keep watch, because you do not know on what day your Lord will come" (Matthew 24:42). If we had known, we would have tried to prepare and unpreparedness will be the downfall of some. I believe God talks to our souls through preaching and teachings of his word, not necessarily a warning or premonition but a reminder that he is coming soon to wake up the Christian believers when we become complacent. If we listen, we can hear Him. Once again maybe his mercies in disguise.

In a twist of irony, my mother had e-mailed my sister and me and then called each one of us kids only a couple of weeks before the accident to tells us to "keep watch." Was He making it known to my mother, or was He just reminding her that salvation is on the line? I don't know what God's purpose was in whispering this to my mother's soul, but it was put on her heart to tell her children. My brother's response to my father was: "I'm not ready. I have to raise Olivia."

The truth is no one feels like they are ready but today might be the last time you hear the alarm clock. Today might be the last time you see your children. Tomorrow might be the last day of work for you. Most people don't stop and think, *What if this is my last day. What if this is the world's last day?* We go about our day as if we will have many more mundane days and that this one is just as normal as yesterday, as we thought on that fatal day. We expect to get up, go to work, come home, and do it all over again the next day. This isn't unknown; this we know. We do this every day, right? Well don't we? I have to say that I felt the same way until December 22, 2008 when I woke up in a hospital waiting room surrounded by family members in disbelief. Unfortunately, I wasn't waking to a *buzz, buzz, buzz.* No mundane day for me, and I am sure none of us were sleeping. When we did arise on December 22, 2008, we were still praying and hoping for a miraculous blessing to come upon our family. Though we expected the worst, we were just unaware of when the worst was going to happen. Situations like this can turn the most optimistic people into pessimists, especially with doctors and medical staff all around saying he isn't going to make it and they are preparing for death and the harvesting of his organs. As human beings, we tend to believe the doctors instead of us putting faith into God's hands. We are trained to believe and put our faith in medicine while trusting that doctors know exactly what is happening and believing they can fix anyone. We believe almost everything they say because they are doctors, right? But how many doctors have been wrong? How many have said to some family, "I am sorry, there is nothing we can do; he just isn't going to make it," just to turn around and see the patient was improving and that they made a miraculous recovery. We rely a lot on medical science to get our facts and the truth, but the real truth lies with God.

Now, my mother is a true optimist and believes that the whole truth and nothing but the truth comes from God, and you can take that as gospel, no pun intended. She is always the optimist, and one of those rare few that don't put her faith in doctors; she puts all her faith in God. She never doubted that God was going to send healing in the way that she wanted healing. She wanted her son to get up and walk away from this. God is faithful to the faithful, right? After all, it is written in Matthew 18:20 (NIV), "For where two or three come together in my name, there am I with them." And there was a flock of people joined together in His name praying over Josh. Christ promises to be with us, as the verse states, but He doesn't say he will concur with us. She would continue to pray for the healing of her son, as we all would, and that God's will be done in this situation, though I know she was really hoping and praying that their wills matched. You just never know what God's will is in the situation that you are desperately praying for. You just pray that His will be done and have faith that this will occur because His will does occur. Just because the end is not what you wanted it to be doesn't mean God's will wasn't done. "Many are the plans in a person's heart, but it is the Lord's purpose that prevails" (Proverbs 19:21 NIV) This doesn't mean that God has left you out in the cold to suffer. It doesn't mean this was punishment. It means His will was done and that there is a purpose. God tells us in Ecclesiastes, "There is a time for everything, and a season for every activity under the heavens: a time to be born and a time to die…a time to weep and a time to laugh, a time to mourn and a time to dance" (Ecclesiastes 3:1-2, 4). If God made everything known to us, wouldn't that make for a boring life? Wouldn't it make it more difficult for us to trust and have faith in God? Wouldn't it make us better sinners? Wouldn't it make us all knowing? Isn't that why we are in the position we are in? Isn't that the apple? We are abiding, faithful creatures that were created in his image to serve Him, not to question His purpose for our lives.

We aren't only made to serve God. God also wants his people to be faithful and trust that he will provide everything needed to survive including hope. "For his anger lasts only a moment, but his favor lasts a lifetime; weeping may stay for the night, but rejoicing comes in the morning" (Psalm 30:5, NIV). It is impossible to know when that rejoicing will happen; you are just to have faith and hope that it will come. I surmise that life is similar to Plinko on the Price is Right; you lay your puck, or several pucks, down one at a time and you let it go. You watch to see where it is going to land. It is unknown at the top exactly where it is going to go; however, you have a great vision and strategy, and you set it all the way to the left and just when it is about to land in the big money slot, it veers off and flops elsewhere. I guess the big difference is God only gives you one life, and it can veer off and come back. It can stay on the exact path you wanted it to, or it can flip, flop, and do circles, but it is really up to God's plan where and when it lands, and that is unknown. However, we do know that Romans 8:28 (NIV) is true: "And we know that in all things God works for the good of those who love him, who have been called according to his purpose." There is always a purpose, despite having plans for our lives, but this went against "my purpose" in life. This seemed to be a blow to the plans he had for his life too. Remember, he wasn't ready. Turns out, there is always joy in the suffering.

It is no secret that this was not how God's original story was to end. This was not the purpose of creation. The original plan was nicely set up in the garden of Eden and then some snake slithered by, and that's all he wrote, or was it? Now, the original plan was changed, and the new plan, unknown, if you will, takes off, because sin was set into motion. But it was never unknown to God. He is omnipotent; it was just unknown to man. Wasn't being "in the know" one of the reasons Eve was tempted and sin entered this world. She wanted to be more like God, to have his knowledge.

> "You will not certainly die," the serpent said to the woman. "For God knows that when you eat from it your eyes will be opened, and you will be like God, knowing good and evil." When the woman saw that the fruit of the tree was good for food and pleasing to the eye, and also desirable for gaining wisdom, she took some and ate it. She also gave some to her husband, who was with her, and he ate it. Then the eyes of both of

> them were opened, and they realized they were naked; so they sewed fig leaves together and made coverings for themselves.
>
> Genesis 3:4-7 (NIV)

The evil cunning devil that now slithers on his belly is very convincing. We have all experienced him, his ways, and how deceitful he is. The one and only good thing I can take from the devil's temptation of Eve and that is this: My mother would have a harder time trying to catch and kill him with a weed eater if he still had little legs and feet.

It would've been difficult, I am sure to live in a place that caused gawking enticement, like the apple tree. Imagine if you will, driving along and all of a sudden a big pothole appears and your car just falls in. That must be similar to what Adam and Eve felt, or close to it. They were just minding their business in Eden, and the snake came along, tempting her with knowledge if she ate the juicy apple. Not just a little knowledge but closer to God's great power and knowledge. It had to be too much to handle for her. *Snake + Apple +Eve = pothole (aka: sin).* I know, I know, again you are thinking, *Didn't God know this was going to happen; therefore, this was his original plan after all?* That is a question I can't even begin to understand or answer. Free will is a nasty thing, isn't it? We, as sinful human beings, tend to think that because we have been faithful, or somewhat faithful, that we would be spared from the trials and tribulations of this world, and when we are not, we become angry, resentful, eat the apple or question God for the situation. Wouldn't you agree that free will causes many of the crosses we bear? After all, God created Adam and Eve in his likeness and gave us free will, so why is it wrong to want to be like him in regards to His knowledge. Eve was probably asking herself that question amongst others. For example: Why couldn't she eat from a tree that was created for their garden? Why would He conceive something so scrumptious for our garden, our home, and tell us it is forbidden? Why would God allow them to be tempted when He made them in his image and beseeched them to be faithful creatures? Hm, maybe that is the answer. He implores us to be faithful creatures and hopes that believers in Him will walk past the apple tree. We assume these temptations should only happen to nonbelievers, most certainly not Adam and Eve. However, history proves that the apple trees of this earthly realm have existed from the beginning of time, and our free will to eat from it has caused a considerable amount of damage and pain.

God never promised Adam or Eve or the world that affliction wouldn't infiltrate our lives; he promised he would give us Himself, His son, and the Spirit to lead us through it. These moments, much like the apple tree predicament, are true tests of faith, and I didn't want to fail because failing may mean not spending eternity with my heavenly Father or my brother. What you learn, if you persevere, is that He is the Father of comfort, He is the Father of strength, He is the Father of blessings, and He is the Father of joy, hope, grace, and mercy. As we grieve, we grieve like sinners, and it seems impossible that these trials and tribulations will reveal a purpose in His plan, but they will. Death is disruptive to the normal balance of things, but in it, there lies hope. Hope for a new and perfect body. Hope for everlasting life. Our hope endures through sufferings to comfort, as

Paul tells us, "And our hope for you is firm, because we know that just as you share in our sufferings, so also you share in our comfort" (2 Corinthians 1:7, NIV).

"There are seldom, if ever, any hopeless situations, but there are many people who lose hope in the face of some situations."
(Zig Ziglar)

As the vigil was held over Josh, we continued to pray that God would allow him to overcome this, but we feared the worst. We worried about what we would do without him. "Can any one of you by worrying add a single hour to your life?" (Matthew 6:27, NIV). I often question how one can have hope and dread at the same time. Maybe because hope is an eternal, internal belief that just never goes away. It is permanently etched into the souls of Christians, and no one can erase it. I believe that eternal hope, hope everlasting is different than "I hope I pass this test." Eternal hope, as Paul talks about in Titus 1:2 (NIV), "Is in the hope of eternal life, which God, who does not lie, promised before the beginning of time." This is the hope that I believe can't burn out in most people. It reminds me of a song I learned as a child in VBS, I think you all will remember, and the chorus goes like this: "This little light of mine, I'm going to let it shine." If you think of hope in terms of this light burning until Jesus comes, then my idea of eternal hope makes perfect sense. You aren't going to hide it under a bushel; you most certainly aren't going to let Satan blow it out; you are going to let it shine till Jesus comes. Simple I know, but childlike faith is simple. As you can see from the song, this is the type of hope that never burns out, and I believe this is what we felt for Josh and what Josh most assuredly felt for himself. Josh knew that he had the grace of God with him and hope of everlasting life, Titus 3:7 (NIV) says, "So that, having been justified by his grace, we might become heirs having the hope of eternal life." Could we hope for anything more?

I can remember the neurologist coming in and addressing the family and simply saying, "There is nothing we can do." Translation: There is *no* hope. The brain damage is just too severe. Translation: It was a hopeless situation. It felt like a hand grenade had been thrown in the waiting room, and we didn't know to take cover. I looked around the tiny little room we were all sitting in, so tiny there wasn't enough seating, and I watched everyone's reactions to the grenade. The realization, for me, was so overwhelming and shocking that I just wanted to scream, "You are lying! You are wrong! Do the surgery anyway and drain the fluid build-up off his brain, and then he will be well! Just give him a chance. This isn't hopeless." But as quickly as she had walked in to tell us it was hopeless, she then, almost ran out and left us alone. I understand that, it isn't the medical staff's job to comfort us, hold our hand and tell us it will be all right or that we will get through this. This is the Lord's job, and He was right on time like normal. God sent in the chaplain after the doctors left that little room. He introduced himself and asked if we wanted him to pray with us.

My dad said, "Yes, and by the way, we are Lutheran." The Chaplain responded, "So am I."

The little things or signs of irony you pick up on later. This was just another sign of His truth. He has been holding our hand all along and comforting us. He knew already that this outcome was a part of his plan. He knew we needed Him, He knew before Josh was born that this would change our lives. God knows everything, even the length of our life as He knew for his only son. "Your eyes saw my unformed body; all the days ordained for me were written in your book before one of them came to be" (Psalms 139:16, NIV). He knew that He would place it upon my heart and soul to write this manuscript, and He knew that I would listen which, in turn, would never have been done without the suffering. He knew the greater purpose of our suffering would also transform the lives around us, because of Josh, just by reading this book, but I didn't know this three years ago. It is written in the book of Jeremiah 29:11(NIV): "'For I know the plans I have for you,' declares the Lord 'plans to prosper you and not to harm you, plans to give you hope and a future.'" I also knew, because of this verse, that, whatever the outcome was going to be, it is for His glory and no one else's. I know that whatever path He chooses for us, the walk will not be alone, and I can count on him that He is always ten steps ahead. There is hope in that assurance. "The Lord himself goes before you and will be with you; he will never leave you nor forsake you. Do not be afraid; do not be discouraged" (Deuteronomy 31:8, NIV).

Finally, we were allowed to go back to his room in the ER and be with him. They were preparing a room in the ICU for him until the family could make some hard choices about harvesting his organs. As I stood near his head, I could see the damage to his skull and, ultimately, his brain. The staff had done a poor job of covering his head, as the injury was still visible. I then had an understanding of the hopeless situation the doctors had been referring to. This was a pretty dark place to be in, but I guess God took Job, the apostle Paul, and His only son through some pretty dark places as well. They all had to bear painfully heavy crosses, so why wouldn't my family and I?

Paul said about Jesus Christ: "I can do everything through him who gives me strength" (Philippians 4:13, NIV). Paul talks about a vision he had, and in this vision, he tells about the thorn that was placed in his flesh to torment him as a messenger of Satan. Paul apparently pleaded with the Lord several times to remove it, and this is what the Lord said, "My grace is sufficient for you, for my power is made perfect in weakness" (2 Corinthians 12:9, NIV). Paul goes onto say in verse 10:

> Therefore I will boast all the more gladly about my weaknesses, so that Christ's power may rest on me. That is why, for Christ's sake, I delight in weaknesses, in insults, in hardships, in persecutions, in difficulties. For when I am weak, then I am strong.
>
> 2 Corinthians 12:10 (NIV)

It doesn't seem like this was a hopeless situation for Paul because Paul knew that we, like himself, could set our hope on the Lord, and the Lord would continue to deliver us from any hopeless situation, which in turn, would make this a hopeful situation, right? So how could my brother lying in ICU be hopeless when hope is revealed though it?

Once Josh had made it to ICU, the family pretty much could come and go as we pleased. The medical staff didn't really hold us to the ICU rules, but we were respectful of the other patients and tried not to fill his room the whole time. We all took turns sitting with him, praying with him, and holding his hand. Josh had many friends that drove more than three hours that night just to be with him and us. They too wanted a chance to see him and to support the family. As we sat with him, the medical staff was in and out of his room, doing what they do: trying to keep Josh comfortable and answer our questions to the best of their ability. I admit, I am a black and white thinker, and I like to have cut and dry answers to everything. I don't like things left up to interpretation, there is a right or wrong answer for every question, in my mind at least. Then, it would be normal of me to have as much information about a situation as I can, especially when it concerns my brother's life. I remember one of the nurses coming into his cubical to check his stats. I wanted to see what the doctors saw on the scans and the tests. I wanted to know why this was hopeless. She obliged me and showed me the scan results and explained to me what I was looking at and why the medical staff couldn't fix him. I definitely saw what they did; however, I clung to a little hope that he was going to be a miracle.

December 21st turned into December 22nd, which then turned into the 23rd. It was Tuesday, but it still seemed like Sunday. In ICU, the days drag on and seem to run into each other. Looking back, there were definite themes to each of these days. The first day, or really eve, was spent with tests and doctors saying it was hopeless, which left us spending the evening in total shock and disbelief. The second day was spent with him in his room, while I know the medical staff were preparing for organ donations and the staff kept him alive and comfortable for that very reason. This was the day that my sister-in-law and our family made the hardest choice of our entire lives: to allow the machines to be turned off and donate his organs so someone else's family could have their hope restored. Finally, the last day for us, of course, was the hardest. We never knew when the medical staff was going to come in and say, "It's time to go." The weather was the worst it had been in years; the area was expecting several inches of ice that day, or night. The staff was waiting for the other hospitals, which were taking his organs, to decide if and when they were making the journey to transport the organs. Saving a life is important, but risking lives to save some, well, that's another issue. Finally, word came that someone would be traveling to get his kidneys in this nasty weather while others decided not to risk their lives.

Here we are now, trying to cram in as much time with him as possible as we wait and as Josh waits to hear, "Well done, good and faithful servant" (Matthew

25:23, NIV). The medical staff is explaining that once they turn the machines off, there is a time frame in which organs remain viable. Essentially, if he didn't stop breathing on his own within ninety minutes, they would bring him back to ICU and turn the breathing machines back on. Sounds pretty horrible, doesn't it? It seemed like an ultimatum to me. I heard: "Your brother either needs to stop breathing so we can have his organs, or he will go back on the machines until he does stop breathing." I can see now what they were saying, but when I was in shock and grieving, my thoughts weren't rational.

Does anyone realize how much discomfort we are really in at this point? Here we are, two days before the world was to celebrate the birth of Jesus, two days after celebrating the birth of my son Jacob, and we are being told, "It is time." What? Seriously? This is really going to happen? Where is God in this? What is God creating? What has happened to our hope? Why is there not comfort?

Saint Paul writes: "We also pray that you will be strengthened with his glorious power so that you will have all the patience and endurance you need" (Colossians 1:11, NLT). These settings in life do generate impatience, weakness, and questioning. It is said there, in verse 11, that strength, patience, and endurance are given to the faithful ones. Paul is spelling it out for his generation that there are all these great things that we have in Christ, if we are faithful. As Paul's writings unfold, it seems that he is consistently teaching that the enduring, faithful servant will find rest. Paul never taught that life would be a cakewalk. Let's reflect.

Even Christ was troubled despite knowing that his Father was going to give him rest. "Now my soul is troubled, and what shall I say? 'Father, save me from this hour'? No, it was for this very reason I came to this hour. Father, glorify your name!" (John 12:27-28, NIV). In truth, we didn't need Saint Paul to caution us that we would be oppressed, but lifted high. Christ instructed us in John 16:33 (NIV): "I have told you these things, so that in me you may have peace. In this world you will have trouble. But take heart! I have overcome the world." Christ declared these things way before Josh was born. Christ proclaimed these things to ensure that, when this happened, we would remember. Remember that He overcame the grave. Remember that we will be given strength, comfort, and hope. Remember that only greatness can come from a hopeless obstacle. How can tragedy be gratifying? This is how: because we can't be severed from the love of our Lord Jesus Christ. "Who shall separate us from the love of Christ? Shall trouble or hardship or persecution or famine or nakedness or danger or sword?" (Romans 8:35-36, NIV).

The apostle Paul was determined to profess to everyone through his teaching and writing that salvation came through faith, not works, and, in conjunction with faith, comes comfort, compassion, and strength to carry on through the trials, troubles, and tribulations. Again, Saint Paul writes:

> Praise be to the God and Father of our Lord Jesus Christ, the Father of compassion and the God of all comfort, who comforts us in all our troubles, so that we can comfort those in any

trouble with the comfort we ourselves receive from God. For just as we share abundantly in the sufferings of Christ, so also our comfort abounds through Christ. If we are distressed, it is for your comfort and salvation; if we are comforted, it is for your comfort, which produces in you patient endurance of the same sufferings we suffer. And our hope for you is firm, because we know that just as you share in our sufferings, so also you share in our comfort.

2 Corinthians 1:3-7 (NIV)

Paul clearly makes this point at different times in his writings. He says Christ will comfort us, however, he announces that if we need to be comforted, it is for our salvation. Moreover, he describes how our suffering should enable us to comfort others as God has comforted us. Saint Paul continues:

We do not want you to be uninformed, brothers and sisters, about the troubles we experienced in the province of Asia. We were under great pressure, far beyond our ability to endure, so that we despaired of life itself. Indeed, we felt we had received the sentence of death. But this happened that we might not rely on ourselves but on God, who raises the dead. He has delivered us from such a deadly peril, and he will deliver us again. On him we have set our hope that he will continue to deliver us, as you help us by your prayers. Then many will give thanks

> on our behalf for the gracious favor granted us
> in answer to the prayers of many.

2 Corinthians 1:8-11(NIV)

Paul expresses, in these last verses, that troubles arise for which we will depend on God, not ourselves, and have faith and hope that we will be delivered time and time again.

These verses were not exactly music to my ears. Why is it, if he is the Father of compassion, that I felt no compassion or peace? Why did it seem as if we would not endure through this? Why did all hope look lost because obviously Paul says it isn't? Well, to explain it, I must refer to Romans 8:6 (NIV): "The mind governed by the flesh is death, but the mind governed by the Spirit is life and peace." Satan likes to put his best game face on when we are the most vulnerable. This could be the point we sink or swim, spiritually. If we believe everything that the world is saying and don't trust in the word of God, our spirits will feel no peace.

In 2 Corinthians 2 (NIV), Saint Paul is writing about why one should forgive an offender. He writes in verse 11, "In order that Satan might not outwit us. For we are unaware of his schemes." The verse may be about forgiveness, but it is true in many situations. Satan believes he can outwit us at any turn and when this jagged turn, approaches us in thick fog, in a torrential downpour, and we can't see the end, Satan is going to jump in with as many schemes as possible because he likes it when there are doubts and frustration. He delights in creating questions, frustrations, doubts, and anxiety. This is his playground in life. If he can lead us out of the sandbox with disappointment, he can lead us down the road of faithlessness and through the woods of doubt, away from our father. Satan whispers in the ears of the human race all day. He tells our hearts lies in hopes it will convince our souls. Satan understands the ways of the world. After all, he is a globetrotter; "And the Lord said to Satan, 'Where have you come from?' Satan answered the Lord, 'From roaming throughout the earth, going back and forth on it'" (Job 2:2, NIV).

Although we suffered with the frustrations and questions Satan was casting at us, God did protect us while sending his comfort and peace. Satan was wrong about that once again. God restored our hope and faith. Our questions were not tests to God about his power or control. There is no doubt that he is a sovereign Lord. The Holy Spirit warns us not to test Him because he has been tested before, and they wandered for forty years, as it was written in Hebrews:

> Today, if you hear his voice, do not harden your hearts as you did in the rebellion, during the time of testing in the wilderness, where your ancestors tested and tried me, though for forty years they saw what I did. That is why I was angry with that generation; I said, "Their hearts are always going astray, and they have not known my ways" So I declared on oath in my anger, "They shall never enter my rest."
>
> Hebrews 3:8 (NIV)

I'm going to put it into my layman's terms: when God allows you to go through the wilderness, don't become callous and disobedient to God when He speaks, unless we desire to end up with no hope, like the believers that Moses lead out of Egypt. Ergo, when they became disobedient: "And to whom did God swear that they would never enter his rest if not to those who disobeyed? So we see that they were not able to enter, because of their unbelief" (Hebrews 3:18-19, NIV). We should learn from their example and aim not to follow by listening to the evils of the world. "Let us, therefore, make every effort to enter that rest, so that no one will perish by following their example of disobedience" (Hebrews 4:11, NIV). If you continue reading through Hebrews, you will also discover that we are told that those of us who are going to be called by heaven should have hope of the forthcoming glory. God says in Hebrews 13:5, (NIV), "Never will I leave you; never will I forsake you." In order to really understand it, I believe you have to walk through it and then turn around and behold it. I have to describe it like someone that climbs Mt. Everest: You don't really notice how far you are ascending, how things are changing, or how magnificent it truly is until you get to the top. The climb up must be very painstaking and tiresome. Some give up, and some have died trying, but some make it to the final peak. Once at the top, you turn around and take it all in: the landscape, the climb, and the journey. You get the real picture. It has to be overwhelming and breathtaking: the pure, raw beauty of this panoramic background that very few manage to see with their own eyes. The journey to the top of suffering may not seem beautiful as you climb that mountain, but I assure you, if you have taken the right path, whether you have fallen over obstacles and struggled with unanswered questions, whether on the soar to the crest you gave up for a moment or just felt defeated but continued on that rise, when you look back at what you have been through, you will realize that Christ carried you like he carried His cross; it then will have been worth the climb, even with the unanswered questions.

I discovered early on that it didn't matter how many questions I had, this was going to take place and soon. They turned the machines off in his room, as a test, while we watched. His breathing became labored to the point I wanted shout at them, "Turn the ventilator back on!" I was scared and upset. It is a horrifying experience to watch someone start to lose life, and I didn't want to see him suffering. I am not sure what the test was to show; it seemed pointless to me. By this time, there were more than ten people gathered around his bed, every one of us that was up there. The room was almost overflowing. My father has been in constant prayer, especially while in his room. We all stood holding each other's hands, including Josh's, as my father led us in repeating the Lord's Prayer and the Nicene Creed. The staff encouraged the family to talk to him and touch him, but they did make it clear that he couldn't hear or feel us. However, referring back to that childlike faith, I believe that every time we prayed with him, God interceded and allowed him to hear us. Maybe, he even participated in the Lord's Prayer with his family for the last time. As we prayed, I had a hold of his foot, and he felt so cold while my mother and Betsy were holding his hands. Then, they came to take him away. Betsy was the only family member allowed to go with him. My mother wanted to be with him too, but the rest of us stood in the ICU area, watching the gurney roll away. It was sort of like seeing the elusive rabbit go down the rabbit hole in *Alice and Wonderland*, however, there was no chatter about being late for an important date because he was right on time, according to God's watch. "Indeed, the very hairs of your head are all numbered" (Luke 12:7a NIV). The elevator was really a door into an unknown world for us, much like the hole Alice fell in to. She encountered new adventures, stressful situations, and felt completely lost, alone, and helpless at times. At the end, Alice had found her strength and might to beat the demons. Nevertheless, Alice woke up, and we had not fallen asleep. As the elevator doors closed, my heart trembled. This would be the last time we would ever see him in this earthly realm. Job 14:4 (NIV) reads: "A person's days are determined; you have decreed the number of his months and have set limits he cannot exceed." It was official; Josh's hope was rising as ours were falling.

It remained fairly silent as we sat with anticipation, waiting for Betsy's return in the empty hospital hallway. We were alone, no patients, no medical staff, just our makeshift waiting room for the last several days. Josh and Betsy's minister, Pastor Ryan, went with her for spiritual counsel and support. Pastor Ryan had been with us for the majority of the time; after all, he was the one that just held the Bible class in which the, now infamous, question was asked: "Why does God take young people?" Pastor Ryan, young like us, took time away from his family and his preparation for Christmas services in the church to be with us. He didn't have to do that, but he wanted to, and we were grateful to have him there. Who else was going to try to answer the hard questions we had. "Why does God take young people?" Most certainly, a layman's answer would not suffice for this one; we needed someone skilled in Gods handiwork to explain to us exactly why this was occurring in our lives. Don't let me confuse anyone; it isn't about why this is happening, death happens. It is about "Why is it happening to us?" I realize that this question assumes we are being treated unfairly.

I understand this isn't any more unfair than the woman that prepares her nursery, enjoys her baby shower, goes into labor, and then delivers a stillborn baby. It isn't any more unjust than a son or daughter that doesn't come home from war. It isn't any more uncalled for than a father and mother that can't feed themselves or their children because there is no work. I don't believe that anyone can give us the real reason for any of these moments in time because we don't know what our sovereign Lord is thinking, completing, or what he is preparing us for. "'For my thoughts are not your thoughts, neither are your ways my ways,' declares the Lord. 'As the heavens are higher than the earth, so are my ways higher than your ways and my thoughts than your thoughts'" (Isaiah 55:8-9 NIV). We know that

He will be glorified through this, and because He is glorified, we too will be glorified,

> The Spirit himself bears witness with our spirit that we are children of God, and if children, then heirs—heirs of God and fellow heirs with Christ, provided we suffer with him in order that we may also be glorified with him.
>
> Romans 8:16-17 (NIV)

We continued in silence as we each secretly counted down the ninety minutes his life was allotted. They told us that he would come back to ICU if he were still breathing on his own after ninety minutes. There was an unspoken flame of hope that Josh would be strong enough to prove them wrong. Miracles do happen every day, and this would be our miracle. Oh, how he will change lives with his testimony! Ninety minutes is a short time to review our thirty-some years together, but be that as it may, ninety minutes is also a long time for your mind to wander and question. What if I would have had the birthday party on a different day? What if they would have taken a different direction home? What if he would have stayed longer at my house? What if, what if, what if. You can drive yourself batty with the "what ifs." If you camp out with the "whys" and the "what ifs," your faith will diminish and become stagnant. When faith dwindles, we fall behind instead of drawing closer to God and drawing from his strength; we will slow down healing and start to question our faith and hope. God tells us, this is not the end, but merely a beginning. Death can't win, death doesn't have the final say, and death will be destroyed. "The last enemy to be destroyed is death" (1 Corinthians 15:26, NIV). God is very clear, when it is all said and done and the trumpet sounds, there will be a new beginning. Christ discloses that this is all just temporary. In a blink of an eye, it will be over, and we will be raised and reunited in the glorious resurrection. We have the hope of this promise. Why? God declares it is so. The end verses of chapter 15 point this out perfectly:

> Listen, I tell you a mystery: We will not all sleep, but we will all be changed in a flash, in the twinkling of an eye, at the last trumpet. For the trumpet will sound, the dead will be raised imperishable, and we will be change…then the saying that is written will come true: "Death has been swallowed up in victory."

> 1 Corinthians 15:51-52, 54 (NIV)

The flame of hope continued to flicker in our hearts. Ask yourselves, if you lose hope what do you have? The answer is nothing.

It seemed like we were hawks waiting for prey while watching the opening to the corridor that led from the elevator. This is the direction that Betsy would come from, and we wanted to be ready. When we saw her walk through the doorway, my sister and I ran to her and held her. While crying, she began by telling us that he remained alive for ninety-one minutes, one minute past the allotted time. It felt as if they rushed her and pastor Ryan out because there were other families, hopeful that their loved one would live because he died, and I guess they did. In order for the organs to be viable in the transfer, there isn't much time. There is a long and careful protocol, including more timeframes, for harvesting organs, and the two of them were now in the way. Betsy would go on to say that his breathing was pretty strong and steady as it reached the ninety-minute mark. He started to labor a bit, I am sure fighting with all his might to stay alive. She said she leaned over and told him, "It is all right, we will be taken care of," and he stopped fighting, "to depart and be with Christ, which is far better" (Philippians 1:23 NIV). The flame of hope, for his life, burnt out for us but lit up for others.

Do you ever wonder as that flame starts to flicker and smolder out what really happens in the end? Science can't truly document or explain the things that happen right before death or after. Do you know you are dying? Is there a struggle with heavenly hosts to stay alive? Do angels accompany you to heaven? Do you immediately have a perfect body? Do you recognize everyone because we will all be family? Do you remember anything from just moments before? What we do know spiritually is that the body returns to dust, and the soul of the believer in Christ goes to paradise, "To be absent from the body is to be present with the Lord" (2 Corinthians 5:8 NIV). The earthly life that was snuffed out is living in the hope of life everlasting, the promise of the Lord, for those that believe. Our hope for everlasting life has now been heightened.

> But we do not want you to be uninformed, brothers, about those who are asleep, that you may not grieve, as others do who have no hope.

> For since we believe that Jesus died and rose
> again, even so, through Jesus, God will bring
> with Him those who have fallen asleep.

1 Thessalonians. 4:13–14 (ESV)

Now here we are, like lost children once again. Where do we go? What do we do? We are left to try to get out of the rabbit hole like Alice. Please, wake us from this horrible nightmare.

Then, we remembered we hadn't slept in days. Since we obviously weren't waking up, we sat around, questioning pastor Ryan for several hours as the ice started to build up outside on the roads. The travel home for all us of was not only going to be treacherous but excruciating. Normally, the travel home would be less than two hours, in good conditions, but we were facing arctic chills.

The ice was thick on the windshields and was continuing to build up. The task of clearing the ice from the windshields turned out to be to daunting. The ice was forming quicker than we cleared it. We did the best we could and headed out. The four-car caravan south began about 9:00 p.m. Betsy and her mother headed out first; Sara and our mother second; my husband, Josh, and I were third; and my father trailed behind us. My father has always felt he should bring up the rear out of protection of his family. The interstate was covered in ice and vehicles driving twenty-five mph tops. I found myself thinking, *Man, what else can happen? Josh dies and we are looking at least a half a foot of ice. It feels like we can't catch a break, and right before Christmas too.*

I can't tell you what desperation feels like, but you know if you have ever been there: Desperate to under-stand, desperate to know why, desperate to just wake up. We needed comfort and we needed it right then.

> For I am sure that neither death nor life, nor angels nor rulers, nor things present nor things to come, nor powers, nor height nor depth, nor anything else in all creation, will be able to sep-arate us from the love of God in Christ Jesus our Lord.
>
> (Romans 8:38-39, NIV)

That is pretty comforting, and I know He was there the whole time. Who else held Josh's other hand for those ninety minutes and beyond.

We continued our travel at a snail's pace. We were texting each other and keeping track of everyone; we didn't need another accident occurring. We decided to follow my sister home to make sure she got there safely. She lived in the middle of nowhere, and in nowhere the roads were much more dangerous. The last hill to her home was so slick that my dad drove his vehicle down and up and then got out and walked down the slick hill to maneuver Sara's van up the hill. Josh and I stayed at the top of the hill, waiting for my mother and father to return. They finally made it back up the hill, and we were off again for another thirty-mile drive. My parents were staying with us. It was 3:00 a.m. It took us six hours to drive seventy-five miles. I was never so happy to see my driveway.

Rest didn't come that morning, and we faced another day, the first day without him. It was now Christmas Eve, the day before the celebration of Christ's birthday, but we didn't feel like celebrating. My parents needed to be with Betsy to make arrangements, and I had to tell my kids what had happened. My oldest child, Faith, had a special relationship with her uncle Josh. She was the first grandchild born, hence, she is the oldest of the cousins. Faith loved him very much; when she was just able to talk, she walked up to him and said, "You are my bestest friend ever." The smile on Josh's face was priceless; it reminded me of the Grinch's face when his heart grew three sizes. Every time he would see her, sometime during the visit, he would say, "Hey, I haven't got a hug from my bestest friend ever," and she would run up and hug him. What a tradition we would all miss. Imagine my distress in telling his bestest friend this thing that would bring the most pain she would feel at her young age. "Precious in the sight of the Lord is the death of his saints" (Psalm 116:1,5 NIV).

Faith is taking a giant step into nowhere, blindfolded, while being fully aware that your foot will land securely

Faith, my daughter, took the news like I had expected: by crying hysterically. At eight years old, she was able to understand what I'd said. It didn't faze Jacob, my five-year-old; the news didn't have an effect on him at all. Death is so abstract to children, especially young children. I wish I were able to accept death like my five year old. It appeared to be much easier than the adult way. I explained that he was with God and that we would see him again in heaven someday. Faith, like a child, isn't that what Christ says we should have? My children just believe that they will see Josh again. They just believe that God and heaven exists. They don't question; they don't doubt. They just have faith that it is true and that there is a God. If we live by faith, it shapes us and changes us. It is written: "Now faith is confidence in what we hope for and assurance about what we do not see" (Hebrews 11:1, NIV). If you question God, then at least it shows that you believe he exists. In Hebrews, it is written that we need to fix our eyes on Jesus because he is the pioneer and perfecter of our faith. The verse continues on and points out that

Jesus suffered what he did so we don't lose heart and grow tired. "Fixing our eyes on Jesus, the pioneer and perfecter of faith. For the joy set before him he endured the cross, scorning its shame, and sat down at the right hand of the throne of God" (Hebrews 12:2). When you put it all into perspective, it makes our sufferings seem so small, but no matter how small, the losses are big.

Jesus also had a big loss with his friend Lazarus. It is obvious by reading John 11 that Jesus cared very much for Lazarus and his sisters. Jesus not only wept at Lazarus's tomb, but he turned around and raised him from that same tomb. It goes to show that Jesus understands grief and pain. It shows that Jesus has compassion. Jesus understands the difficulties in this life, and Jesus cares for my family; however, he wasn't going to raise Josh from the dead like his friend Lazarus. In John 11:23-24 (NIV), "Jesus said to her, 'Your brother will rise again.' Martha answered, 'I know he will rise again in the resurrection at the last day.'" Little did she know that soon Jesus would bring her brother out of the tomb. Jesus was completing one of his miracles so the people would have faith in who he is: the Son of God. There are many times I wished that Josh was going to be another Lazarus. After all, doesn't Jesus care for Josh's family like Lazarus's family? Doesn't Jesus have compassion for us as well? I wanted to have faith that this would come to pass, but it just doesn't happen that way anymore. Jesus doesn't visibly walk the earth in human form anymore. Only with us in the spirit. That isn't to say that miracles don't happen; it just wasn't happening for us on that day. I believe like Martha, and she is right. "I know he will rise again in the resurrection at the last day" (John 11:24, NIV).

Jesus has a vast knowledge of what it is like to be human because he was born to a virgin mother. He has felt tremendous pain; just look at the crucifixion. This is pain that no one can fathom. There is no comprehension of what that may have been like for Jesus to experience or for his family and friends to endure. They all had faith that they would see him again, but it didn't stop his mother, Mary, from crying or from missing her son. First Thessalonians 4:13 (NIV) says, "Brothers and sisters, we do not want you to be uninformed about those who sleep in death, so that you do not grieve like the rest of mankind, who have no hope." What does that verse really mean? Doesn't it seem to suggest that those of us with faith, Jesus's family and ours alike, shouldn't grieve like the average Joe, that we should grieve, but grieve knowing that faith has saved us, and by grace we will all be resurrected? Isn't that what Martha was saying in John 11:24? Martha was saying she has faith that on the resurrection that her brother would be raised. Isn't that where mankind should be striving to be at the end of the race? It is okay to be sad, grieve, and cry, but find peace from knowing that faith will lead us home to everlasting life. There is the promise that joy will come from this suffering.

Philippians 3:14 (NIV) says it clearly: "I press on toward the goal to win the prize for which God has called me heavenward in Christ Jesus." Faith in everlasting life is God's greatest promise, and even though death may seem to win out every time you are at a visitation or a funeral, it isn't true for believers. In 1 Thessalonians 4:16-17 (NIV) it reads:

> For the Lord himself will come down from heaven, with a loud command, with the voice of the archangel and with the trumpet call of God, and the dead in Christ will rise first. After that, we who are still alive and are left will be caught up together with them in the clouds to meet the Lord in the air. And so we will be with the Lord forever.

Death is not the end for the believers in Christ.

Children's Bible stories are full of believing characters. As kids, like Faith and Jacob, you couldn't help but just have faith, especially after just hearing about stories like the great flood. As it is written in Genesis 6:9 (NIV), Noah was a great believer. "Noah was a righteous man, blameless among the people of his time, and he walked faithfully with God." It is probably safe to say that he did whatever God asked and that he followed God's direction to a T. God told Noah exactly what to do, what kind of wood, how long and high, how many decks and doors. God told Noah to bring his family and two of every creature, male and female. Now, that is some strong abiding faith. After the flooding was over, God promised Noah that he would never flood the world again and told Noah to look into the sky and that the rainbow would be the sign of His promise. Rainbows are still out today; it is a promise that God continues to keep. Every young child and adult knows the promise, whether they believe it or not, and are amazed by their beauty when they see one because they don't come with every storm or rain. It is a reminder that God loves us, and that, no matter how bad the storm, we should have faith that there will always come a bright new day.

> I lift my up my eyes to the hills-where does my help come from? My help comes from the Lord, the Maker of heaven and earth... The Lord will keep you from all harm—he will watch over your life; the Lord will watch over your coming and going both now and forevermore.
>
> Psalm 121 (NIV)

The day after the accident, I volunteered to drive my parents home to gather some things and leave a closed sign on the business door. On our way, my mother looked up into the western sky, and there it was. Shining so beautifully on a bitterly cold, windy morning was the promise from God: a rainbow. At this point, I was amazed at the oddity of this miraculous thing; there was no rain, no warmth, just cold bitter temperatures and wind. It followed us all the way to our destination.

I haven't seen the part in the Bible were God promises a rainbow only in the spring and summer months, have you? Then you might think that it wouldn't be unusual to see a rainbow, a sign of His promise, in the spring, summer, fall, or winter? God didn't say his promise would only appear during certain times of the year. If you saw a rainbow, say, around December 22nd, the dead of winter what would you think? Would you think, it must be some kind of anomaly? Would you wonder if God does send his promise in the winter? Would you project that this was specifically for you and your family and that it would all be okay? On December 22, 2008, that bright, beautiful promise shown in the sky. The earthly explanation is that it is a sundog; as you know, the world seems to have an explanation for everything. However my mother had faith that it was God's promise to her that her son was going to be okay. It was a promise all right, but we, of course, wouldn't know that until later. The truth is, God keeps his promises for those that are faithful. And that promise would come true for Josh soon.

Faith is much like the rainbow: a promise from God. Those of us that keep the faith will see the promises fulfilled, even though we doubt at times. While in the midst of suffering, trial, and tribulation, like Paul and Job, we must still have faith that God keeps his word. Even the disciples doubted, at times, when they were with Jesus. Think about the time Peter and the disciples were in the boat. In Matthew 14, Jesus was walking on water, and the disciples were frightened; they thought Jesus was a ghost. Jesus had to call out to them and identify himself so they wouldn't be terrified of this person walking on the lake. Peter doubted this for a second, and said to Jesus, in verse 28, "Tell me to come to you on the water." Jesus then said to him, in verse 29, "Come." Peter, apparently, obeyed because, all of a sudden, the wind picked up, and a frightened Peter, again, started to sink. While sinking, he cried out for Jesus by saying, in verse 30, "Lord, save me!" Guess who saved Peter. Yep, Jesus Christ himself, and as Jesus was saving Peter's life from the water, He said to him, in verse 31, "You of little faith… Why did you doubt?"

Why do we doubt? Is that a loaded question? It seems obvious for the disciples that for as long as they had been with Jesus he works in miracles and blessings. He raises people from the dead. He healed the blind and lepers. He fed the five thousand with minimal loaves and fish. He died and rose again like He said He would. However, it wasn't a no-brainer for them; Peter and the disciples, for a split second, doubted that He could walk on water. Then again, in Mark 4:35-41(NIV), the disciples thought that Jesus was going to let them drown. They were so scared that they woke Jesus up, and Jesus rebuked the waves and it was calm. Jesus again asked them about their lack of faith, "Why are you so afraid? Do you still have no faith?" So it doesn't amaze me that we could doubt, for a split second, that we would find strength, peace, and healing in the midst of our suffering or tribulation. It doesn't surprise me that we sometimes lack the faith it takes to see that this is all for His glory. We only get to read about these miracles that Jesus performed and are supposed to have faith that it happened just as we have read it. The disciples got to experience it, and they lacked faith at times.

In contrast to this, Abraham, against all hope believed the promise to him from God: that he would be the father of many nations.

> Without weakening in his faith, he faced the
> fact that his body was as good as dead—since

he was about a hundred years old—and that Sarah's womb was also dead. Yet he did not waver through unbelief regarding the promise of God, but was strengthened in his faith and gave glory to God, being fully persuaded that God had power to do what he had promised.

Romans 4:19-21(NIV).

Man, that is powerful. Even when Abraham was old, and it looked as if Sarah wasn't having any children, Abraham still kept his faith that God would come through on His promise. I don't need to go into the story of Abraham, do I? Though it does remind me of another song I learned as a child that goes like this: "Father Abraham had many sons and many sons had Father Abraham. I am one of them and so are you, so let's just praise the Lord." We all should be like Abraham: strong, persevering, and unable to give up on our faith. No matter how old or long he waited, he had faith that God would keep his promise to him, and he did. We aren't waiting to be the father of many nations, but we are waiting for the glory of God to come shining through as He promised. We are waiting to see God's face as He promised. We are waiting to be reunited with our families that have died and will die, believing in Christ Jesus. Jesus said, "Did I not tell you that if you believe, you will see the glory of God?" (John 11:40, NIV).

The glory of God is difficult to see in suffering. I am sure that I am not alone in that sentiment. It seems apparent that even the disciples would agree with me. Maybe I should say that the glory of God, in this particular situation, is hard to see. God knew that we would suffer from this great loss in our lives, but he also knew this was for the glory of Him, even if we didn't see it. There is faith that this is fact and that God would never allow something to happen that wasn't ultimately for His glory. As human sinners, we don't always see it this way, at least at the beginning. Apostle Paul writes:

> Through whom we have gained access by faith into this grace in which we now stand. And we boast in the hope of the glory of God. Not only so, but we also glory in our sufferings, because we know that suffering produces perseverance; perseverance, character; and character, hope. And hope does not put us to shame, because God's love has been poured out into our hearts through the Holy Spirit, who has been given to us.
>
> Romans 5:2-4 (NIV)

I am not suggesting that anyone should or could jump up and down when dealing with grief or any other suffering. What I am alleging is that, through hardships and sufferings, we as believers in Christ should be growing in our relationship with Him, and eventually, through our faith in Jesus Christ, we shall see the glory revealed to us. That is the hope. Maybe, instead of asking why and questioning, we should be asking: how could I use this to glorify God? How can God's glory shine through me because of this suffering? "Consider it pure joy, my brothers and sisters, whenever you face trials of many kinds, because you know that the testing of your faith produces perseverance" (James 1:2-3, NIV).

I have a hunch about what perseverance means. This isn't a word I use often; it is a behavior I can see in myself. It shows up in the Bible enough that I should have a clear understanding of it. After a Google search, this is what I read: "Steady persistence in a course of action, a purpose, a state, etc., especially in spite of difficulties, obstacles, or discouragement." As of June 20, 2011, this was Dictionary.com definition of *perseverance*. What was fascinating was the added definition below it. The theological definition revealed this: "Continuance in a state of grace to the end, leading to eternal salvation" (Dictionary.com, June 20, 2012).

Wow, again, that *hope* thing. If we had nothing to pursue, we wouldn't move anywhere. After reading dictionary.com, I can only presume, at least theologically speaking, we should be pursuing eternal life. Without faith, we step into this giant world and have no real idea of what our feet are going to land on. Without faith, we just think that this is the way it is, and people will suffer for no good reason. Without faith, we wouldn't believe we needed to pursue anything but worldly possessions. Without suffering, which pushes us to pursue eternal life, we would just be sitting around like those non-believers pursuing this sinful world.

However, because I am a believer, I wasn't alone waiting in a hospital for word. I was a believer when I was at home telling my children. I was a believer when I was standing next to the casket. I was a believer as I listened to TAPS play off in the distance. I was a believer when they handed my sister-in-law a folded flag, and I will be a believer when I watch his daughter walk down the aisle without him. Because of faith, I knew I wasn't alone, I wasn't lost, I wasn't left behind, and I wasn't forgotten. Because of faith, I have the hope of everlasting life. Because I have faith, I know someday not only he, but also we, will rise again. I am learning that, through the suffering process, I have been building faith and perseverance to win this race. I am learning that, through this suffering, God is being glorified through many different outlets, and I know there was a reason God spoke to my soul to write, for the glory of Him. Calamities hit saints and prophets too for their salvation. Don't go it alone. Ask yourself: What are you pursuing?

"So with you: Now is your time of grief, but I will see you again and you will rejoice, and no one will take away your joy." (John 16:22, NIV)

One thing I have learned from this suffering is that I am not defined by my situation and that I am not alone. I cannot change the circumstances, but I can evolve as I move through them. At the other end, as I reflect, I realize that Christ defines me and not the experience. I am not a grieving Christian, but I am a believer in Christ that mourns the loss of her brother. The latter has a different ring to it, doesn't it? Yes, the heart wrenching experience was debilitating in all facets of life. It seemed as if time just stopped and we were suspended there in that moment, not being able to move; yet, the world wasn't. The world kept on turning, and the clock kept on ticking. I am not sure any of us really knew what day it was or cared. However, I was acutely aware of what was going on around me probably more than ever before. I was in slow motion, but nothing else was. It was soon Christmas, two days after Josh was called home, and no one in the house felt like celebrating Christ's birth. My parent's neighbor had essentially made the whole Christmas dinner for us. This was the day that my parents were to receive their last gifts given to them from the three of us, knowing this was heartbreaking for me. Betsy had chosen to spend Christmas with Olivia alone, but I headed over to get the gifts they had bought to bring back to my parents. This was a very difficult drive to and from the house that, just four days before, my brother was living in. Calamities can change every aspect of our lives in an instant. And it can feel like your joy was sucked out, but it is not.

The first holiday without him, and it just happened to be Christ's birthday. My heart fought with grief and guilt. The guilt is for mourning a life when we are supposed to be celebrating the most important life: Jesus. I think that this was a true test of love for us. We could have cancelled Christmas for the year, but we didn't. We could have stayed at home, curled up in our beds, but we didn't. It wasn't our greatest celebration, but we managed. We clung to every memory of Josh that we could. Like Linus clinging to his blanket, we were just trying to hold on, but our little secure world had been shattered. Not many words were spoken. All the traditional stuff came and went. The children ripped into the gifts, as normal, though my parent's faces weren't normal as they opened up the gifts we bought for them. Their faces were priceless and unforgettable; there was so much love, pain, and great emotion in their faces from the gifts. Here they were, opening gifts that were partially from a boy they would be burying the next day. The love that filled the house Christmas day was undeniable, probably stronger felt than any other time in our lives: love for our family, love for each other, and love for Josh. Love for a baby boy that had been born to man so many years ago, yet was God's own son. "And now these three remain: faith, hope and love. But the greatest of these is love" (1 Corinthians 13:13, NIV).

Honestly, despite the hardship, faith, hope and loved remained in our family. My earthly father in no way, shape, or form was going to let our family fall apart, and neither was my heavenly one. As a family, we would sit in that church, listen to the service and bury Josh with love, grace, and honor. We would stand as a family and play the hand that was dealt to us and do it with hope while we suffered. We would hold firm and faithful on the solid path that Christ had put before us, when He paid the ultimate price, and we would continue to walk that path in the word, until the end. "Your word is a lamp for my feet, a light on my path" (Psalms 119:105, NIV).

We had some time as a family to be with Josh at the funeral home before the procession of mourners started to come through. My mind often wandered off to daydreaming about what he was doing in heaven, and what it is like in heaven, while still being in a state of shock. Who was he talking to and spending time with? Did he find our brother Todd and our grandparents? Was he introduced to the first patriarch of our bloodline to ever enter America? Many of these daydreaming thoughts are what kept me preoccupied and focused. That is an oxymoron, isn't it: preoccupied and focused? Focused on getting through the visitation and service by staying preoccupied. I needed to be strong when the grieving visitors came through to give their condolences.

I tried to stay away from thoughts that would cause me pain, and hence, make me an utter wreck. I wasn't wondering what Betsy and Olivia or my parents were going to do without him. It was easier for me to stay preoccupied with what Josh was doing, and what it is like to be in everlasting life. I knew if my mind got off track that I would be concentrating on the trouble this world gave us, and I didn't want to do that. I didn't want to become angry and resentful like the world expected. I searched pretty hard for peace during the services. It seemed if I was able to distract my mind from the obvious that I was better able to cope, at least for the moment. Really, visitations seem like a place people go to visit with family and friends they haven't seen in years. This is not the right place to catch up on old times.

Luckily the weather had finally taken a turn for the better. It was now unseasonably warm for the day after Christmas. I guess this was nice for the mourners that stood in line waiting to say their good-byes to a closed casket. The line seemed to stretch for miles out of the funeral home; it was as if they were camping out at a ticket booth to buy the best concert tickets for the Rolling Stones. It was so warm the day of the visitation and funeral, the windows in the parlor were open, and those who had long sleeves on were overdressed. How interesting that three days prior we had bitterly cold wind chills and inches of ice and snow. I suppose God has a sense of humor.

Prior to the services, we all picked out pictures of Josh, and the funeral director had them put into a video that ran nonstop throughout the visitation. The visitors came and went as they watched pictures of our family playing on the screen. I didn't want to see those pictures. I wanted to see him. I wanted him to be alive and not on film. I wanted to be sitting at home enjoying the Christmas holiday with family instead of mourning, but the video kept playing, and the people kept coming, and the world kept turning. When you assess it, all I really have now is a constant video playing in my head of him. "Very truly I tell you, you will weep and mourn while the world rejoices. You will grieve, but your grief will turn to joy" (John 16:20, NIV). What a phenomenal idea, this idea of grief to joy. Not exactly the easiest concept to wrap your mind around while in the midst of weeping. Jesus says that there will come a time when we don't weep and when we will be joyful. It seems this might be difficult when you miss someone so much. The truth is, if you miss them so much, you miss the idea of grief to joy, you miss what Jesus is saying. If you miss what Jesus is saying, you only see what the world wants you to see about death, and what the world says about death has no bearing with God. Remember this from John 3:16 (NIV): "For God so loved the world that he gave his one and only Son, that whoever believes in him shall not perish but have eternal life." Let's try not to grieve like sinners but grieve like a believer. When you grieve as the Bible instructs you too, you know the upcoming joy is heaven.

As you continue through the book of John you come upon chapter 16. In chapter 16, Jesus has a conversation with the disciples. Jesus made a statement to them, telling them that they won't see him in a "little while," and then, in a "little while," they will see him again. It would appear as if the disciples were pretty confused by this statement, and they kept inquiring what He meant by "little while." It is almost like the Cat in the Hat riddle isn't it? It doesn't exactly make a lot of sense, but it has some meaning or purpose behind it. "In a little while you will see me no more, and then after a little while you will see me" (John 16:16, NIV). I get why they may have been feeling like they just stepped out of a Dr. Seuss book. Of course, we all know what Jesus was talking about in chapter 16; He was saying simply that He would die and that they would mourn and grieve, even if others didn't. However, have peace in knowing that we will meet again, on that fateful day and we will rejoice in heaven together. "I have told you these things, so that in me you may have peace. In this world you will have trouble. But take heart! I have overcome the world" (John 16:33, NIV). Jesus is letting the disciples in on a little secret, so to speak. Jesus is saying, "Because I am going to die, you will live." He is saying that the world will bring havoc to our lives, but we should have peace in knowing that He died for us so that we will live. He is saying grieve, weep, and mourn, but one day we will see him; we will see the glory of God and we will see Josh, again, because Christ lives in us, and we live for Christ. Everything done is done for the glory of God. This is for His glory.

The dreaded day came for the funeral service and the burial. We waited in the back room of the old Lutheran church that Josh was a member of to start that long painful walk toward the casket. Envision Dorothy on that long walk following the yellow brick road, focused on her final destination: Oz. What a long, lonely walk to the front of the church, behind my parents and sister-in-law, while my eyes were fixed on the casket at the front of the church. That path wasn't yellow; it was stained in tears. Once we were all seated, the service starts. I can hear, in the background, the organists playing "How Great Thou Art." The grief was like a wave from hurricane Irene, it just washed over the packed sanctuary and left a wreckage of debris among the pews. Unfortunately, FEMA couldn't clean up this emotional mess; only Christ could. I can't imagine that anyone would say that this process is a cakewalk, and I have been to many funerals for friends and family, but there was something unique about this one. Pastor Ryan stood at the pulpit in the front of the church like a seasoned minister and comforter from God. He spoke eloquently and it was about our Father, not Josh.

Pastor Ryan didn't base his sermon on Josh and what kind of man he was. He based his sermon on God and what kind of God He is: the kind of God that sends His son to die for Josh, for all of us. One statement I remember well that Pastor Ryan said at the pulpit was, "Satan is a liar." I must refer to John 8:44 (NIV), when trying to support this point for the readers. "He was a murderer from the beginning, not holding to the truth, for there is no truth in him. When he lies, he speaks his native language, for he is a liar and the father of lies." This is very true. We didn't need him to tell us that, but let me put this into context for you. Pastor Ryan started the sermon with Adam and Eve and ended the sermon with Christ dying so we can live. Somewhere in the middle, he explained, "Satan is a liar." He lied to Adam and Eve, and he is lying when he tells us that our lives are ruined. He is a liar when he tells us that Christmas will never be the same. He is a liar when he tells us that we will never be the same, or when he whispers, "Your God killed your brother." Satan is a liar, and that statement has rung through my ears for almost three years now. "Liar, Liar, pants on fire." So, I guess the sermon may have been a little about Josh but a lot about Christ and the hope for heaven. If you were there, you knew who Josh was, but I suspect that, in the packed house, there were people there who didn't know who God was but did when they left.

Martin Luther once wrote, "All the cunning of the devil is exercised in trying to tear us away from the word" (*What Luther Says*, Ewald Plass, St. Louis Concorcia Pulblishing House, 1959). Lucifer will go to the ends of the earth or hell to try to lure each and every one of us to his side. He is cunning, and humans start to dance with the devil even without knowing it sometimes. Satan is very elegant in his charms. He is skilled at causing feelings to flare up, good or bad, and he is very competent at twisting the situation so we view it differently in order to cause us to sin. And pull us from Christ. We react or act on feelings, and if we behave badly by making poor choices, then that foothold starts. Mourning is a perfect time to lure you away, it is a weak point for most. "In your anger do not sin… and do not give the devil a foothold" (Ephesians 4:26-

27, NIV). This was a difficult verse to comprehend as you hear TAPS being played, and you see the perfectly folded American flag being handed to your sister-in-law, or when you look into your three year old niece's eyes and see your brother, but you know that is all you get to see of him anymore. Anger is difficult to repress; however, sin doesn't have to come from it.

Joy and anger are complete opposites, and here I am telling you that we should be rejoicing in the things to come. I didn't say it was a sin to be angry and neither does the above verse. The verse was intended to explain what one does with their anger could determine whether Satan can convince us to follow him or not. Nowhere does it say that it is all right to have feelings of anger, and it is not proper to be sinful because of it. It wasn't all right for me to call the woman that ultimately caused Josh's death on the phone and make degrading comments to her because she made a mistake. It was not appropriate for me to be angry and post negative things about the woman's character on Facebook. It was not kosher to make judgments about her and her lifestyle out of frustration and anger. It was acceptable to be angry that the situation occurred and that sin had entered our little world with a big wallop. Then it was fair to be angry that sin exists. Without any doubt, I believe that Satan then turns around and feels angry that this or that human wouldn't be lured away from Christ. Maybe we stole his pleasure for the day, but Satan can't steal our joy. We can grieve as believers and not sin, or we can grieve as sinners. It is written in John: "So with you: Now is your time of grief, but I will see you again and you will rejoice, and no one will take away your joy" (John 16:22, NIV). But if you are on the wrong path, joy will never come.

"For the world was built to develop character, and we must learn that the setbacks and griefs which we endure, help us in our marching onward." (Henry Ford)

In the aftermath of any destructive situation, if you don't get up and move forward, you essentially check out of life. Remember that old saying "When life gives you lemons…"? Well the world would like you to make lemonade. The world would like you to pull yourselves up by your bootstraps. The world is wrong, the lemonade is bitter and the bootstraps are broke. When Life is full of tangled, enmeshed strings, lives, and issues, detangling them is a process, and sometimes it isn't our earthly job to detangle. These strings and messes, as we see them, are there for a reason. In other words, we aren't always meant to understand why this string is connected to this seam or that seam. God has purposely orchestrated this life, and if we don't understand, this is more than likely a sign that we never will and that it wasn't our purpose to understand, so don't try to detangle it, it will leave you frustrated. We don't get all the information in this life.

I have several ministers in my life, mainly because my family all attend different Lutheran churches. My sister's minister, Pastor Osborne, once gave her an analogy while she was struggling to have an understanding of this loss. It goes something like this:

> Life is like a handmade quilt. All we see is the bottom with frayed ends and strings entangled or enmeshed with different lengths. This look is somewhat chaotic and doesn't really have a pattern; however, Christ sees it from the top. At the top, it is a beautifully sewn quilt that flows and makes perfect sense.

I love this analogy, and it really does make perfect sense, doesn't it? Once I started to put one foot in front of the other, I could understand completely what point he was making. "By faith we understand that the universe was formed at God's command, so that what is seen was not made out of what was visible" (Hebrews 11:3, NIV). We knew that these strings that were dangled and tangled in our lives all connected to the glory of God.

Most of us take baby steps trying to untangle what we can to move toward recovery. Hearts aren't healed overnight, and minds don't rest weeks later. Almost three years have gone by, and my mind still wrestles with thoughts of Josh daily and questions how God's glory will prevail. There are times that the thoughts are so obsessive that I feel like I am going crazy. At times, the moments, and sometimes the days, just knock me off my horse, and I feel like I can't get back on. However,

I keep marching forward with the help of Christ. I found that, at the beginning, it took a lot of strength to pull me out of bed in the mornings and get me going. I went back to work after two weeks, but I didn't feel up to it. The unfortunate part of mourning in American businesses is that America's businesses have this grieving policy of two to three days, and that is if you are full time. Part timers don't typically get any paid time off to grieve. I just happened to have some extra time for the holidays so I could be gone for two weeks.

My first day back, I was in session with a client and just started to cry; I couldn't hold it in. Here I am, still trying to find the bottom of the quilt before I can even think about untangling it, yet I am expected to help others untangle theirs. I felt horrible because they are here for me to counsel them over their emotional/ behavioral issues, and I was the one crying over my own. Man, imagine what might have been going through the client's mind when his counselor broke into tears. I am not sure you can preface a session with "By the way, my brother just died, so excuse my emotional state." I had to close my door after the client left and get on my knees and ask for strength. I have had to do this a lot in the past couple of years. Paul writes: "Strengthening the disciples and encouraging them to remain true to the faith. We must go through many hardships to enter the kingdom of God" (Acts 14:22, NIV). It sometimes makes me wonder just how many hardships is enough to enter the kingdom. If you think about it, this verse is similar to Romans 5:3-5 where it addresses how sufferings, in the end, produce hope through character building. Sufferings and hardships are definite character builders and faith builders. This idea of pushing forward to the final goal through suffering is again mentioned in James 1:12 (NIV), "Blessed is the one who perseveres under trial because, having stood the test, that person will receive the crown of life that the Lord has promised to those who love him." There should be no doubt by now, I am making a point: suffering will lead to hope and push us onward toward the end goal. Nowhere can I find in God's Word where it says, "Sit around and remain stagnant." I have been unable to find where God's Word implies that the human race should rely upon earthly things for strength and leadership through hardships. Absolutely not, the word is clear: lean upon Christ and he will move you forward toward that the everlasting goal.

> Not that I have already obtained it, or have already become perfect, but I press on in order that I may lay hold of that for which also I was laid hold of by Christ Jesus. Brethren, I do not regard myself as having laid hold of it yet; but one thing I do: forgetting what lies behind and reaching forward to what lies ahead, I press on toward the goal for the prize of the upward call of God in Christ Jesus.
>
> Philippians 3:12-14(NASB)

Keep in mind, Josh's death wasn't the only hardship we had to endure; it was just the primary hardship with many secondary hardships to come. Until you suffer this, it is difficult to describe the intensity of the loss and all the little losses that follow, which cause suffering, almost like a ripple effect.

Most days, it still felt like we were living in the middle of tornado alley while the F5 winds continued to blow without ceasing, and each new day seemed to bring a new hardship. First, it was Christmas without him, and accompanying that was the empty chair at the Christmas dinner table. We have plenty of family to fill that chair, but there were many holiday dinners before anyone was allowed to sit at the end of my parents table. That was his chair and has been since our family grew. This little itty-bitty thing caused much suffering and pain. Other hardships arose like who was going to mow my parent's lawn when they needed help. He had specific chores in his own household that now Betsy had to absorb or that abruptly ended. Who had inherited the job to call my twin sister and me very early in the morning, even before my mother, on our birthday? Who was going to help my parents run the business they shared together? These were some of the little hardships that blindsided me some days. These things that caught me off guard would bring about more suffering, but someone had to step in. When these needs, that don't seem to have a resolution to them, appear, know that God will provide. "And my God will meet all your needs according to the riches of his glory in Christ Jesus" (Philippians 4:19, NIV).

I mentioned before, my parents shared a business with Josh and Betsy. My father worked at the business full time, and Josh would come in every evening, after his fulltime job, and on the weekends. There were many,

many hours put into this business by both Josh and our
father. There were many weekends that my husband and
I would come help when they needed it. Imagine having
a business partner that suddenly stops being in business with you. The slack has to be picked up somewhere
and by someone, but it's just another hardship. Isn't that
what Satan would say? God has a way of meeting the
needs of His people, and He stepped up and enlisted
my husband to run this business with my father. All of
our needs are taken care of at the cross. See how God
steps in and makes His presence known in a setback?
Just when you think the suffering is never ending, God
brings the resolution, we march onward, and as I see it,
Satan's team loses again. First Peter tells us to be aware
of the evil one and his tactics to persuade us that God
isn't quite who we believe he is. Satan can be very convincing at times, especially when we are in the middle of
a setback; these are some our weakest points in life. But
remember what the Bible says: Satan is a liar.

> Be alert and of sober mind. Your enemy the
> devil prowls around like a roaring lion look-
> ing for someone to devour. Resist him, stand-
> ing firm in the faith, because you know that
> the family of believers throughout the world is
> undergoing the same kind of sufferings. And
> the God of all grace, who called you to his eter-
> nal glory in Christ, after you have suffered a lit-
> tle while, will himself restore you and make you
> strong, firm and steadfast. To him be the power
> forever and ever. Amen.
>
> 1 Peter 5: 8-11 (NIV)

This verse simply seems to suggest that we resist what Satan is whispering in our ears, resist what Satan is whispering to the heart because he is constantly reminding us of our hardships, of our sufferings, and he plays upon our weaknesses. Satan is looking to attack at the Achilles's heel, the weakest point. He is always on the prowl, like an owl waiting for his next meal. Satan's lot in life is to lead us astray and to tell us how our hardships and pain are from God. Satan is good at disguising himself as helpful, but in reality, he is trying to tear us away from Christ. Resist Satan and continue to stay strong and firm in Christ because Satan is a liar, and God will provide. He is the father to the children without fathers. He defends the widows. He is the provider.

As I have described, this expedition is full of ups and downs, much like a roller coaster. There are days when you know that you have kept your hands and feet in at all times, and you just wish the ride would come to a complete stop so you can get off. However, it never seems to stop. Just when you think you can pick up the march, the coaster takes off again. This is not a strange or alien concept, this is the way of life on earth, though some drops are steeper than others, which only means a longer, harder trek back up. Humans are used to this mountain climbing by now. That doesn't prove all hope is gone, it just shows that, in this setback, the one set of footprints in the sand might be there longer this time. It can be frightening, facing a changed world. Circumstances will change. People will change. Surroundings will change, but the Bible leads you to the one sure thing: "I the Lord do not change" (Malachi 3:6, NIV). The world as we knew it was gone and this new one brings with it fear. Change is a process and a scary one, but because Christ loves us, He will carry us through. We shouldn't be afraid because He loves us, "There is no fear in love. But perfect love drives out fear, because fear has to do with punishment. The one who fears is not made perfect in love" (1 John 1:18, NIV).

"Blessed are you who weep now, for you will laugh." (Luke 6:21, NIV)

There can't be anything better than that final and finest blessing which will be bestowed upon man, eternal life "And I heard a voice from heaven saying, 'Write this: Blessed are the dead who die in the Lord from now on.' 'Blessed indeed,' says the Spirit, 'that they may rest from their labors, for their deeds follow them" (Revelation 14:13 NIV)! My great friend and beloved pastor would say, "Death is the final healing." However, along the way, we find that we are blessed with things while here on earth even if we don't always see them. These will never equal the final blessing but they satisfy while here. Christ is full of blessings and has a habit of doing so to his faithful sheep. It would seem that the more faithful you are the more abundantly these blessings flow from God. I talked earlier about Job and how he was blessed more in his later life than at the beginning. It is written that this is because he was faithful to God even when his wife said that he should turn his back. Even when his life was made difficult, Job did not retreat. In the end, "Job died, an old man and full of years" (Job 42:17, NIV). He was blessed for his faithfulness to the Lord so I know that God completes this for all that are faithful to Him. It is written in James:

> Brothers and sisters, as an example of patience
> in the face of suffering, take the prophets who
> spoke in the name of the Lord. As you know,
> we count as blessed those who have persevered.
> You have heard of Job's perseverance and have
> seen what the Lord finally brought about. The
> Lord is full of compassion and mercy.
>
> James 5:10-11(NIV)

God wants us to be faithful throughout our lives, not just in good or bad times but in all times, like His abiding Job. It is easy as human sinners to not rely as much on God when things seem to be going well; this is the *up* time of that roller coaster. When that coaster starts to fall, this is when people also fall to their knees, even if we have neglected our relationship with God for years. When suffering hits a God-believing Christian, that Christian usually falls to their knees. The wonderful part is, even when we have left Christ at times, Christ has never left us. He has continued to listen and hasn't turned his back on us. That in itself is a blessing. The real question here is why don't we stick it out in good and bad just like Job? Why is it that, when things are going the opposite direction than we would like, we rely heavily on God. The answer is pretty clear, I think. It is because tribulation and sin robs us of peace and joy, so we turn to all we know. We know how to lean on the Lord in bad times. Wouldn't it, then, make sense too, when we have peace and joy, lean toward Christ and thank Him for these blessings as well? Maybe, when we become less attentive to God is when God starts to ponder ideas that will bring us back. When I say ideas, I mean trials and tribulations. When His sheep go astray and wander from the herd, something or someone has to bring them back. Just a hunch, but why do you think shepherds have sheep dogs? Once again, the sheep will become faithful and the blessings will start to flow.

When we talk about blessings, we have to review the Beatitudes in Matthew 5. These are eight blessings from Christ, from the Sermon on the Mount. Matthew 5:4 (NIV) says: "Blessed are those who mourn, for they will be comforted." Think about all the reasons we mourn. We don't just mourn the death of somebody; we mourn the loss of a job, a pet, a move, a friendship, relationships, and many other things. Christ doesn't only comfort those that grieve over death of a loved one; He comforts all of us that mourn no matter what we have lost. If we, as Christians, are suffering, we, as Christians, will be comforted. He said in Matthew 11:28 (NIV) "Come to me, all who labor and are heavy laden, and I will give you rest." It is a great relief to know all we have to do is lean on Him and we will find peace. Christ wants us to persevere through suffering; He doesn't want us to struggle, but to persevere, we must have comfort in knowing. "Blessed is the one who perseveres under trial because, having stood the test, that person will receive the crown of life that the Lord has promised to those who love him" (James 1:12, NIV). This is the most beautiful blessing of all.

Blessings aren't haphazardly given away, I am sure. There comes some work in it all, faithful, abiding work. My parents raised the question after his death,

"What are we going to do about this business?" It is now just my dad that is running this business, and he obviously will have some difficulty doing it by himself. This is not a one-man shop. In retrospect, it may have been a blessing that that my husband and I had spent many weekends helping out when Josh was alive, so the choice seemed obvious. Josh, my husband, without hesitation, stood up and said he would come help. "Carry each other's burdens, and in this way you will fulfill the law of Christ" (Galatians 6:2, NIV). I wholeheartedly believe that Christ was already preparing my husband, during those many weekends, to run this business with my dad. Many are the things you can see and put together in hindsight. Remember that chaotic-looking quilt? Well, sometimes, it makes sense along the way. Josh, my brother, was training his replacement on those weekends; what a revelation that has been for me. The once clear path our lives was one has been compromised by the fork in the road.

My husband was well aware that this new part-time job would be keeping him from spending time with us, but his choice wasn't based on inconvenience; his choice to stand up was based doing the right thing. You protect and help your family when needed. It has been almost three years, and he still drives an hour and a half to and from the family store on the weekends. My husband's helpfulness to my parents reminds me of Matthew 25: 34-40 (NIV), and because of this, I know he is blessed by Christ because of his loyalty.

> Then the King will say to those on his right, "Come, you who are blessed by my Father; take

your inheritance, the kingdom prepared for you since the creation of the world. For I was hungry and you gave me something to eat, I was thirsty and you gave me something to drink, I was a stranger and you invited me in, I needed clothes and you clothed me, I was sick and you looked after me, I was in prison and you came to visit me." Then the righteous will answer him, "Lord, when did we see you hungry and feed you, or thirsty and give you something to drink? When did we see you a stranger and invite you in, or needing clothes and clothe you? When did we see you sick or in prison and go to visit you?" The King will reply, "Truly I tell you, whatever you did for one of the least of these brothers and sisters of mine, you did for me."

What Josh has done for my parents, he has done for Christ. It is very clear in Scripture about how God views the importance of loving and helping your neighbor and doing well regarding fellow believers. It is written in Galatians 6:10 (NIV): "Therefore, as we have opportunity, let us do good to all people, especially to those who belong to the family of believers." Josh has been a blessing to my parents and the business has flourished even more since my brother has been gone, he would be amazed. This is all heavenly, not earthly. These are blessings that God has bestowed as a reward for faithfulness through this tragedy.

It's not easy for me to look at the situation we have been in and say, "We have been blessed after the death of Josh," but as you can see, it is the truth. By no means do I want to imply that Josh's death was a "good thing" for our family, because that isn't the case. We lost a love in our life, however, because of our family's perseverance and loyalty after this loss, the Lord has been generous. This much, to Satan's surprise, I would guess, did not destroy our family. It is stated: "We are hard pressed on every side, but not crushed; perplexed, but not in despair; persecuted, but not abandoned; struck down, but not destroyed" (2 Corinthians 4:8-9, NIV). This verse, I think, describes perfectly what we were feeling at the time, but we keep running the race because, first and foremost, we are all aware of the final blessing that He will have bestowed unto us when we finish this race. First Timothy 4:10 (NIV) says: " That is why we labor and strive, because we have put our hope in the living God, who is the Savior of all people, and especially of those who believe."

Now, I stand at the end of the proverbial tunnel—you know, where the light is located—and look back, I see so many other blessings, not just the ones I have already mentioned. Sometimes, things are difficult to see when they are under your nose; they can just seem so little that you don't view it as a blessing. I have a different perspective on things in general since his passing. Things aren't so little anymore, and they have meaning and purpose. I often hear a phrase said on the Christian radio station I listen to: "Have you seen God today?" I can count many little things that have happened that most wouldn't even recognize as a blessing, or God, too many to talk about. Yes, most days I have seen God, but most importantly, today I recognize Him. I see how strong and independent my sister-in-law has become since his passing. In the blink of an eye, she was left with a three year old and a life alone. And like losing a limb she had to learn how to compensate for what was lost. This had to be a demanding obstacle to overcome, but she did it. Let me say that she probably persevered more than any of us. Remember, Christ says he will take care of the widows and the fatherless, and he has. Since then, Betsy has found new love, remarried, and Olivia once again has a father in her life. Josh would be proud. Christ says, "I will not leave you comfortless: I will come to you" (John 14:18, NIV). He has kept his promises to us.

Second Chronicles 15:7 (NIV) reads, "As for you, be strong and do not give up, for your work will be rewarded." God seemed to be rewarding our family even before the beginning and the blessings continued to flow. How much more could God bless one family? Well, since you asked, let me tell you. Soon after the death of my brother in December 2008, we found out in late January 2009 that we were expecting our third child, due in October 2009. My husband and I had been praying for another child for quite a while, and God chose to bless us at this time in our lives, after miscarrying and just weeks before Josh's death. It does seem that God's plan doesn't always make sense to us, but it does to him. It is almost comical, isn't it? My sister and brother-in-law were shocked when they found out, in July of 2009, that she was pregnant with their fourth child. I suppose I am not even sure that I truly understood the magnitude of all the blessings at the time, but when you look back at a situation in your life, because another situation causes you to do so, you discover that you, now, have a new understanding of it that you never had before. Not only does it give you a little peace, but it makes you chuckle. Some things really are just heavenly, and not earthly, and you can't dispute that. These have been some of the beautiful gifts He has given since the loss, but you can't ignore or deny the ones that have always been there in our lives.

> Each of you should use whatever gift you have received to serve others, as faithful stewards of God's grace in its various forms. If anyone speaks, they should do so as one who speaks the very words of God. If anyone serves, they should do so with the strength God provides, so that in all things God may be praised through Jesus Christ. To him be the glory and the power for ever and ever. Amen.

1 Peter 4:10-11 (NIV)

At times I have this tugging sensation on my heart and this whispering in my ear that I have come to know only as God, and I felt the need to reach out to others. I decided that I needed to follow Him and try to help other mourners find some peace, like the peace that I have received. As far as I am concerned, the only way to find that peace is through Him. As I searched the internet, it suddenly dawned on me that this area really needs a Christ-centered grief support group. One of the gifts that God has given me, which is also my career, is to be a counselor, so a grief support group would be a perfect fit for me, a thirteen-week Christ-based, program created by people that have been through suffering and made it out to the other side with God's help. I went to my pastor and discussed my vision with him, and he decided to purchase the program for the church. We implemented it in our Lutheran church.

Paul talks about serving with the gifts God as given to you. In Romans 12:6-9 (NIV), he says,

> "We have different gifts, according to the grace given to each of us. If your gift is prophesying, then prophesy in accordance with your faith; if it is serving, then serve; if it is teaching, then teach; if it is to encourage, then give encouragement; if it is giving, then give generously; if it is to lead, do it diligently; if it is to show mercy, do it cheerfully."

I felt that this was part of my calling, part of a gift I should share, and it was just another blessing from his death, but this time, it was a gift to others. Because he died, we are able to reach out and help others as Christ would want us to do. Paul also writes in Romans: "Share with the Lord's people who are in need. Practice hospitality... Rejoice with those who rejoice; mourn with those who mourn" (Romans 12:13-16, NIV).

"Daughter, your faith has healed you. Go in peace and be freed from your suffering." (Matthew 4:34)

"I thank Christ Jesus our Lord, who has given me strength, that he considered me faithful" (1 Timothy 1:12, NIV). Imagine, you wake up one day, and out of nowhere, you discover that you have an inner peace and strength that is indescribable. There is this joy, deep down inside, that you can't explain. You come to realize that this can only be from God. Maybe, the best way to describe it is something like verse 27 from John 14: "Peace I leave with you; my peace I give you. I do not give to you as the world gives. Do not let your hearts be troubled and do not be afraid." This peace is the Holy Spirit that dwells within, the Holy Spirit that was sent by the Father, himself, in Christ's name. Peace and understanding is not something I thought I would ever gain from this, but because I am a child of God, I know that it was always there. "Therefore, since we have been justified through faith, we have peace with God through our Lord Jesus Christ" (Romans 5:1, NIV). When you continue reading though this chapter in Romans, you read how Paul also tells us that we should be looking forward to, and telling about, the Glory to come, but here is the kicker, and I think I mentioned this before: we should also glory in our sufferings. This verse from Romans substantiates my claim of inner peace. My pastor recites this every Sunday in church: "The Lord bless you and keep you, the Lord make his face shine upon you and be gracious to you, the Lord turn his face toward you and give you peace." (Numbers 6:22-27)

I know I am still suffering, but I know the joy and peace I have, I know the understanding that I have and the desire that I have to finish this race we call life, despite the stinging obstacles.

Some may perceive all this chaos in one's existence as though God placed it there. I reassure those people that this isn't the case. Yes, God is sovereign, which means He is in control, but He doesn't create chaos in our lives. Sufferings aren't meant to be chaotic by nature. It is just how we perceive it as human sinners. First Corinthians 14:33 (NIV) says, "For God is not a God of disorder but of peace." Again, lets reflect on our friend Job. Satan had to ask permission from God test him, and in a similar passage from Luke 21 31-32 (NIV), "Simon, Simon, Satan has asked to sift you as wheat. But I have prayed for you, Simon, that your faith may not fail. And when you have turned back, strengthen your brothers." Clearly, in this case, Satan had to ask permission to tempt Simon Peter as well. When we are withstanding sufferings, it is obvious that it is because sin has entered this world and not because God wants to wreak havoc in our lives. Because of sin, God allows suffering for His glory. Make no mistake, God will use the suffering for his purposes, which is always good, but it isn't a direct curse from the Lord.

Remember, the Lord is always right and just. He will use it to transform us and make everything new.

As we bear sin and the disorder of this world, we search for peace and a way out of the man-made chaos: evil. Peter tells us in Romans that God will take care of Satan and that we will be left with peace and grace. "The God of peace will soon crush Satan under your feet. The grace of our Lord Jesus be with you" (Romans 16:20 NIV). Saint Paul also acknowledges, in 1 Peter 4:12-14 (NIV), that it is normal that we all undergo these trials and sufferings:

> "Dear friends, do not be surprised at the painful trial you are suffering, as though something strange were happening to you. But rejoice that you participate in the sufferings of Christ, so that you may be overjoyed when his glory is revealed."

We should all rest assured that God is in control of the universe and every chapter of our lives. Satan cannot simply do as he pleases and run amuck in our lives. The trials and tests that come to God's people are only those that He allows, and since He allows them, he will also bestow comfort if you wait. "Wait for the LORD; be strong and take heart and wait for the Lord" (Psalm 27:14, NIV).

One of the hardest chapters in life is starting a new one. It may seem as if we are starting a new one every day, or just with each suffering, because we are truly changed people from them. Every day, you turn the page, not knowing what is ahead, trusting in the Lord to lead you down the path in which you are supposed to be on. Have no doubt that He will "guide our feet into the path of peace" (Luke 1:79, NIV). Isn't peace what we truly desire? Think about it, you can meet people that are in some of the most undesirable situations, yet they have peace about it and are not full of worry or anxiety. "Cast all your anxiety on him because he cares for you" (1 Peter 5:7, NIV). If we become preoccupied with worry, we are no longer focused on the final outcome. We are not expressing or giving our anxiety to Christ because if we had, we would have peace and not worry. It is said in Matthew 6:33-34 (NIV):

> "But seek first his kingdom and his righteousness, and all these things will be given to you as well. Therefore do not worry about tomorrow, for tomorrow will worry about itself. Each day has enough trouble of its own."

Pretty simplistically, we are being told to focus on the solution and pray about the problem. "In my anguish, I prayed to the Lord. He answered my prayer and took my worries away" (Psalms 118:5, NIV).

Viktor Frankl, a holocaust survivor, was an Austrian neurologist and a psychiatrist. His book *A Man's Search for Meaning* chronicles his experience as prisoner in the concentration camps and his ability to find meaning for existence, which enabled him to continue living. Viktor lost his wife, his brother, and both his parents during this time. He and his sister were all that remained of his immediate family. Viktor writes, "The truth—that love is the ultimate and the highest goal to which man can aspire. Then I grasped the meaning of the greatest secret that human poetry and human thought and belief have to impart: *The salvation of man is through love and in love*" (pp. 56-57). He continues on page 123 "Spiritual life strengthened the prisoner, helped him adapt, and thereby improved his chances of survival."

Viktor truly understood the less than desirable conditions he was in and how suffering affects the individual's emotional, physical, and spiritual life. Now, granted, one might say he had an unfair advantage to the mind and its afflictions simply because he was a psychiatrist and a neurologist. However, to understand that men have their breaking point in all these facets doesn't take a neuroscientist or psychiatrist, it takes a human being. He managed to be able to exist and find meaning in such atrocities through suffering and spiritual power, not through being a doctor. Frankl concludes that the meaning of life is found in every moment of living; life never ceases to have meaning, even in suffering and death. I have no doubt that Viktor was a great psychiatrist and had a great understanding of the human psyche after his experience, but I have no real idea of his true opinions of Christ. However, it seems his understanding of love and a spiritual existence is what ultimately helped him find meaning and, dare I say, peace.

The time will come, as it did for us, and I am sure for Viktor, that laughing will occur. The time will come for rejoicing and being joyful. The time will come when there is peace and understanding. Please don't be confused or mislead about understanding. I will never understand the loss of Josh and the reasons it had to happen. The understanding I have gained is that there is a purpose; there is a holy purpose that is greater than me, and I am not privy to it. Philippians 4:7 (NIV) states: "And the peace of God, which transcends all understanding, will guard your hearts and your minds in Christ Jesus." And He has done so with peace and acceptance. Acceptance isn't easy, but I have come to know that there is a time for everything under the heavens. As it is said in Ecclesiastes 3:1-8 (NIV), there is

> "a time to be born and a time to die… a time to weep and a time to laugh, a time to mourn and a time to dance… a time for war and a time for peace."

We are not victims, we are children of God and God's children receive peace, comfort, and aren't forsaken by their Father. "I will lead the blind by ways they have not known, along unfamiliar paths I will guide them; I will turn the darkness into light before them and make the rough places smooth. These are the things I will do; I will not forsake them" (Isaiah 42:16, NIV). He will provide the peace even in the rough places. I am reminded of Matthew 11:28-30 (NIV):

> "Come to me, all you who are weary and burdened, and I will give you rest. Take my yoke upon you and learn from me, for I am gentle and humble in heart and you will find rest for

your souls. For my yoke is easy and my burden
is light."

We can find rest or peace even in the worst of times
through Christ himself. We can have peace knowing
that this isn't the end of the world, just merely a hurdle
along our journey to life eternal.

When we lack peace and understanding, sinners
reach for relief in other ways. Gambling, drugs, alco-
hol, sex, pornography, or any other vice that gives us
contentment. The fact is, the world loves immediate
gratification, and when situations give us pain, the first
thought is, *What will help relieve this pain*, whether
physical or emotional. The emotional discomfort lasts
longer and is more difficult to alleviate. Americans
spend a lot of time trying to "make it" in this world,
and we lose sight of our ability to cope. We lose sight of
what is important in life. We lose sight of the end goal.
It isn't different with pain and suffering because we try
to escape the affliction any which way we can. Peace
does not come from the world or the devil, and though
it may seem as if we are getting our needs met, I assure
you we are not. Things feel good in the moment but
lose their effectiveness in the long run. The devil knows
our weakest points and he takes advantage of those
weaknesses. I will once again mention that Paul urges
us in 2 Corinthians 2:11 to beware because Satan tries
to outwit us, and we aren't aware of his tactics. Satan
will insert any worldly temptation in our path that he
thinks will sway us. We already, as the human race, con-
centrate on what the world can do for us instead of
what Christ has proven he can do: heal. "What good is

it for someone to gain the whole world, yet forfeit their soul?" (Mark 8:36, NIV). Why waste our lives trying to pursue ungodly/earthly things, which will ultimately never heal us emotionally or bring us peace, and then spend eternity regretting it? Don't spend everlasting life away from the presence of God because you were unable to find the peace you needed in Christ while on earth. Saint Paul writes in 1 Peter 5:

> Be alert and of sober mind. Your enemy the devil prowls around like a roaring lion looking for someone to devour. Resist him, standing firm in the faith, because you know that the family of believers throughout the world is undergoing the same kind of sufferings. And the God of all grace, who called you to his eternal glory in Christ, after you have suffered a little while, will himself restore you and make you strong, firm and steadfast. To him be the power for ever and ever. Amen.
>
> 1 Peter 5:8-11(NIV)

"God is not what you imagine or what you think you understand. If you understand you have failed." (Saint Augustine)

If you have a vision of who God is and think you have this spiritual thing figured out, well my friend, I am here to tell you that you have estimated wrong, and you should reconsider where you are in your relationship with God. The wisdom of God isn't something that we can understand, even if we think we deserve to know. When we start guessing what God is up to, we start to lose sight of the big picture. We stop listening to God's insight, and we jump off without the truth, and then we transform into frustrated believers. It is written in 1 Corinthians 1:19: "I will destroy the wisdom of the wise; the intelligence of the intelligent I will frustrate." Is that not accurate? Ponder it for a moment. In any situation that outwits us, isn't it usually about how we are unable to interpret God and what he is doing in His great wisdom? The human race was never meant to be privy to the plans of God; the majority of the plan is hush-hush. The part of the master plan we are allowed to see was all ultimately written under the supervision of God, Jesus, and the Spirit. All the information we need to know is at our fingertips. If you want to be enlightened, I encourage you to go out and buy that best seller; it is known as the Bible. If God wanted us to see the big picture, He would have laid it all out for us in Genesis while He was creating the world or while Adam and Eve were betraying it. We can't rely on our eyes and have faith that what we are seeing is all there is. This is just a tiny, miniscule part of the plan. The bigger plan has yet to be seen by the living. I believe 1 Corinthians illustrates the point I am trying to make: "so that your faith might not rest on human wisdom, but on God's power" (1 Corinthians 2:5, NIV).

Let's face it, as we reflect on Adam and his lovely wife, Eve, once again. The two of them just couldn't believe and trust in God or that what He was telling them was the whole truth and nothing but the truth, so help them God. What He wasn't letting them in on was the knowledge that He considered off the record. It seems as if good ole Satan was able to outmaneuver the two of them. If Adam and Eve would have just been able to project into the future, maybe they would have read the instructions given to us in Ephesians 6:10-17 (NIV) where we were told that we should not be fooled by Satan or any dark, devilish schemes. These verses advise us that our battle is against the influences of this dark and shady world and also against the spiritual fury of evil in the heavenly dominion. Not only does Ephesians speak to us about our plight, but in conjunction with that, we are also directed on how to win the battle.

> Therefore put on the full armor of God, so that when the day of evil comes, you may be able to stand your ground, and after you have done

> everything, to stand. Stand firm then, with the belt of truth buckled around your waist, with the breastplate of righteousness in place, and with your feet fitted with the readiness that comes from the gospel of peace. In addition to all this, take up the shield of faith, with which you can extinguish all the flaming arrows of the evil one. Take the helmet of salvation and the sword of the Spirit, which is the word of God.
>
> Ephesians 13-17 (NIV)

We know today that they didn't look toward the future, and they let their faith be tested by a smooth-bellied charmer. I am pretty certain, after the apple calamity, Satan sat back, took a breather, and reveled in his win against God. In my mind, I have an image of him in a recliner with his feet up smoking a Cuban cigar while congratulating himself on a well-played game. However, in all actuality, we know he didn't win; it was just a skirmish in the war of good and evil. Devotees to Christ know the prince of darkness will never take the grand prize. God has better arrangements for that little devil. But even knowing all of this, we are bewildered when God grants Satan's attacks to materialize with His followers.

It may also appear as if wars are waged against his disciples more often than others. That is probably true. Let me illustrate. Why wage war against non-believers? What does Satan have to gain by brawling with a non-believer? They don't usually believe in him either, so he has them on his list already. Doubters would just take the stance that the world dealt them a bad hand. The Christians would know that the bad hand was dealt, subsequently, because of the sin in the world. Understand, Satan wants to claim victory over the believers. He has already conquered the atheists and agnostics, whether they know it or not. Satan wants us to question and doubt the wisdom of our Father, which could enable him to throw a pitchfork into the scenario. He needs the believers on his side and will stop at nothing to gain our trust. The evil one goes against the wisdom of God and tries to convince us to follow suit. If Lucifer can bamboozle and sway us, he can deceive us into believing that God doesn't exist or that God is not love. If there is a sheep that strays and is never found again, where do you suppose that sheep will spend eternal life? As a goat and Satan knows that. He pushes harder with the sheep to change them to goats. Matthew conveys the description of sheep and goats adequately:

> When the Son of Man comes in his glory, and all the angels with him, he will sit on his glorious throne. All the nations will be gathered before him, and he will separate the people one from another as a shepherd separates the sheep from the goats. He will put the sheep on his right and the goats on his left.
>
> Matthew 25: 31-33 (NIV)

Basically, it comes down to one question and one choice. It isn't whether we have life eternal or not; the question is, if we will choose to inherit it as a sheep or a goat. The evil one may try brainwashing, but even he knows and he accepts it. "You believe that there is one God. Good! Even the demons believe that—and shudder" (James 2:19, NIV).

Satan has no wisdom, but his ignorance is disguised easily with temptations and earthy desires.

> "The one who sows to please his sinful nature, from that nature will reap destruction; the one who sows to please the Spirit, from the Spirit will reap eternal life. Let us not become weary in doing good, for at the proper time we will reap a harvest if we do not give up."
>
> (Galatians 6:8-9, NIV)

Doesn't this speak to us and tell us that Christ is aware of the pleasures of life, positive and negative? However, it notes that as long as we follow the path of the Lord, and not the evildoers, that we will reap the benefits of eternal life. I am going to let you in on a secret, if you weren't aware already, evil also has a master plan. It is for us to start relying on the sinful world for our answers. It isn't for us to put down our shepherd staffs and pick up a saber and the armor of God to protect ourselves and our families.

Evil wants us to depend on him to be led through. Satan wants us to curse God and be fearful while becoming frustrated with every quiet God moment spent on our knees instead of resting assured that we are right where we are supposed to be. If we falter when he is done working his voodoo in our lives, and on us, Lucifer will drop each and every one of us like a hot potato. Remember that game when we were children?

We couldn't wait to toss that hot potato to the next guy. The evil one would deny us in a crowd. He wouldn't defend or protect us in a court of law. He would turn around and stab us in the back to succeed. He has no knowledge, truth, or wisdom, only lies. He has no ability to help us fight back, and he wouldn't be nailed to a cross and take the burdens of us because he loves us. He uses us to get what he wants and then it is over. We are left to fend for ourselves at the crossroads of choice: the choice to immorality and destruction or the road to righteousness. Once again, here comes one of those truths for those of us that walk by faith and not by sight:

> For though we live in the world, we do not wage war as the world does. The weapons we fight with are not the weapons of the world. On the contrary, they have divine power to demolish strongholds. We demolish arguments and every pretension that sets itself up against the knowledge of God, and we take captive every thought to make it obedient to Christ.
>
> 2 Corinthians 10:3-5 (NIV)

We fight the evils with the power and wisdom of Jesus and his word. This is the only way to combat the wars against us. We stand firm and strong in the word of the Lord so the evil spirit can't penetrate our breastplate. When you find yourself at that crossroads, my suggestion is wear the breastplate of the Lord, as it is written in Matthew 6:33a (NIV): "But seek first his kingdom and his righteousness."

Finally, you ask, "Wasn't the death of my brother frustrating? Didn't it feel like a battle had arisen? Didn't it seem as though this shouldn't be materializing in our lives?" The answer is yes to all of the above. Darn right it was baffling, disheartening, and even discouraging. We had no control, ourselves, therefore, we felt we needed to rely on someone's wisdom, but we couldn't rest on human insight or common sense. Common sense and humans couldn't explain it any better than we could. We only feared the situation because we were assessing it from the human perspective. No human can understand God's mind-set from earthly ideals. The questions came about only for the reason that we couldn't perceive why He was allowing the strife. Simply stated, we needed to be confident in God's knowledge. How often do we conceptualize the wisdom of any situation while in the depths of it, if ever? "What no eye has seen, what no ear has heard, and what no human mind has conceived" (1 Corinthians 2: 9, NIV). That is His knowledge. We have no conceiving, no comprehension of this great wisdom revolving around us. Our eyes can't see it, our ears can't hear it, and our minds can't embrace it. It makes no sense, yet it makes complete sense. "No, we declare God's wisdom, a mystery that has been hidden and that God destined for our glory before time began" (1 Corinthians 2:7, NIV). Who would of thought that wisdom could be so mysterious and complex?

"Most people are far more prone to let the bad experiences shape their views than the good ones." (Rick Joyner)

I recently had a conversation with my mom, and I made a remark to her that sometimes I feel cheated. I feel cheated that we didn't get to spend the rest of our life with him. I feel cheated because he won't get the opportunity to watch his daughter go to kindergarten or walk her down the aisle. I feel cheated because he won't be able to be my big brother anymore. I could continue with the disservices to this world from his death, but that is only when I am stuck in the "world's point of view." Trust me when I say there are moments and days that I wallow in these ideas, but soon I rediscover that these are my quicksand days; they suck me in and pull me down quickly. I find myself on my knees somewhere alone praying for peace and tranquility to pull me from the quicksand. This is the juncture I hate to be at. Like a plane going down, it is a quick descent, and you are there before you know it. When you nose-dive into loneliness, sorrow, and defeat, it can leave a path of destruction and pure exhaustion.

Most people will let grief overwhelm them and swallow them up in that quicksand for months or even years. There are people in this world that are still suffering immense pain after losing someone thirty years ago, but these have to be the people who have never had hope or who have lost all hope. These are the people that have turned their backs on God and have listened to everyone but the Spirit. The Spirit of truth is all we need. The world is wrong and will betray us every time. Our perspective should come from the cross, not from the universe or the cosmos, not the views of Oprah, Dr. Phil, The Doctor's, not Barbara Walters, not QVC, and certainly not Sylvia Browne or President Obama. None of these singular, influential individuals or programs can help us with their views. Even if they worked together as a whole, they couldn't help us. See, they too are of this world and haven't got the solution. If they did, we would have solved the world's problems, and they wouldn't be getting paid the big influential bucks to hypothesize the solutions of this world one hour a week or on a two hour Saturday night special. Remember when Geraldo Rivera was opening Al Capone's vault? There was so much press and excitement, but once it was opened on national TV, the world was let down. It was empty; there was nothing in it, no answers. That is a lot like what it is to follow the human perspective: empty promises and hollow answers. The world has no truth, just empty answers from a standpoint that doesn't have any bearing. John 4 states:

> They are from the world and therefore speak
> from the viewpoint of the world, and the world
> listens to them. We are from God, and who-
> ever knows God listens to us; but whoever is

not from God does not listen to us. This is how we recognize the Spirit of truth and the spirit of falsehood.

(John 4:5-6, NIV)

I don't want to mislead anyone by assuming that these individuals I spoke of do not belong to the family of God, I am merely making an argument that the world's problems, or John Q Public's problems, can't be solved in an hour talk show or by buying the best new gadget. They also won't be unraveled by calling 1-800-psychic or even by the signing of a bill into law. "See to it that no one takes you captive through hollow and deceptive philosophy, which depends on human tradition and the elemental spiritual forces of this world rather than on Christ" (Colossians 2:8, NIV). The Spirit instructs our soul with the heavenly view through guidance from the Bible and through church while the worldview penetrates our mind through social networking, news, and media.

"Do not conform to the pattern of this world, but be transformed by the renewing of your mind. Then you will be able to test and approve what God's will is—his good, pleasing and perfect will."

(Romans 12:2, NIV)

Primetime has evolved throughout the years to violence, sex, music, and foulness. The limited programming from years ago was all family-oriented and godly. Where do you think our frame of reference comes from? We develop these viewpoints from infancy through our family, friends, news, media and TV. Oh yes, let me not forget social media like Facebook, MySpace, and Twitter. So tell me this, with all these worldly answers, how can one still be suffering as if it occurred yesterday, thirty years later? If they have the heavenly perspective, they wouldn't be. How can two people experience the exact same circumstance and have completely different reactions to them. Take for example, that same person that has suffered for thirty years. I would presume they are angry, bitter, and have been unable to find any meaning or peace from their agony. This is in contrast to the person that is coping thirty years later. This person may look like someone that is peaceful, accepting, and comforted. These landscapes look quite different, don't they? It is our choice in how we view our circumstances and the way we cope.

It is suggested in Philippians 4 that we protect ourselves in all situations with the help of God, but most importantly, we must protect our hearts and minds because we are swayed by the world's perspective, the status quo.

> "Do not be anxious about anything, but in every situation, by prayer and petition, with thanksgiving, present your requests to God. And the peace of God, which transcends all understanding, will guard your hearts and your minds in Christ Jesus."
>
> (Philippians 4:6-7, NIV)

As you can see, Christ, in these moments, continues to ask us to lean onto him, not with our own understanding but on His, as it is said in Proverbs. I would conceive this as meaning we should be reading our Bibles, talking to our ministers, attending worship, and kneeling on the floor with our hands folded. You can't read this verse in Proverbs and interpret it as saying, "Lets go ask Jerry Springer." Reality TV has infiltrated our lives and has grown in leaps and bounds over the recent years. God didn't create reality TV, He created reality. There is a show for everyone, every women, man, child, weight loss, and physical challenge. The list goes on and on. Most of this programming is trying to sell you solutions to the issues at hand, in your life, but it's just another way the world has tried to run our lives. On reality TV, you can find a wife, a husband, train your child to behave, lose weight, win money, run a race against others and so on. If you win the final race or challenge, you also win money, double win. That is the allure: solve my problem and pay me for it while giving me notoriety. Money makes the world better. "For the love of money is a root of all kinds of evil. Some people, eager for money, have wandered from the faith and pierced themselves with many griefs" (1 Timothy 6:10, NIV).

This nation has developed into a nation of families that don't know how to get back to basics, and we stumble over lies and misnomers. Matthew states this: "Woe to the world because of the things that cause people to stumble! Such things must come, but woe to the person through whom they come!" (Matthew 18:7, NIV). Christ may not solve your problems immediately or the way you think they should be solved, but I guarantee He is the key that will unlock the door to grace, fulfillment, blessings, and heaven.

> "Our conscience testifies that we have con-
> ducted ourselves in the world, and especially
> in our relations with you, with integrity and
> godly sincerity. We have done so, relying not on
> worldly wisdom but on God's grace."
>
> (2 Corinthians 1:12, NIV)

We need to depend on the grace of God to get us through, knowing that we never walk alone. Believing that He has gone before us and made the path safe for our treading. "The Righteousness goes before him and prepares the way for his steps" (Psalms 85:13, NIV). Once more, let's return to the example of the thirty years of immense pain verses the thirty years of healing. If I were the wagering kind, I would bet that the person struggling is still viewing their circumstances through the world's eyes and just doesn't know or remember Christ's promises.

If you review the history of people that have suffered, there are many names that come to mind. Let take into account Helen Keller for a moment. She once wrote in an essay called *Optimism* (1903). "The world is full of suffering; it is also full of overcoming it." Her suffering and pain lasted many more years, but her healing lasted more than thirty. Envision what it must have been like for Helen to be able to see and hear for the first nineteen months of her life, and then out of nowhere, her senses were taken from her due to illness. This was a circumstance that was completely out of her control. Much like the car accident that took the life of my brother. I am sure, even at nineteen months, that it was a struggle, especially after having the ability to hear and see. The world as she knew it was changed forever. It must have imitated a thief in the night, the way these things were snatched from her. Now, Helen was sentenced to a life of silence. She could no longer hear her mother's voice or get a glimpse of her family. I am a mother of three, and I know how my two-year-old reacts when she sees or hears me. That tiny person gets excited, her eyes light up as she runs toward me, waiting for my touch. This is a delightful experience for any mother, even Helen's mother, though she was denied this beautiful exchange forever after the illness. I am confident they all learned to adapt and accept the change; however, it had to be distressing. No longer could she react to any sights and sounds, at least through conventional measures, but again, you learn to adapt. I believe there is one word that best describes this nineteen-month-old's circumstance, and that word was *frightening*.

Now, not having the ability to be comforted by your mother's voice must have been difficult in the beginning. This is the age in which our ideas of the world around us are greatly shaped and formed, and in our later years, we hone these ideas and perspectives. Of course, this is where I need to interject and add that God had a plan for her from the start, even before she was born. Jeremiah 1:5a (NIV): "Before I formed you in the womb I knew you." God knew He would mold her into a great women, leader, and activist. God new her view of the world would be forever changed and that it would not hold her back. God whispered in her ear and into her soul that she would overcome this suffering, and she did. Whether Helen knew it was God or not isn't my place to assume, but it seems that God was using her limitations to change lives and He was the only one that knew what was in her heart. Helen never saw her mother with her own eyes again. She never looked out onto the ocean and saw the splendor of it all, or at least she didn't like I would.

Helen graduated from Radcliffe with a bachelors of arts. Helen became an author and gave speeches and lectures. She became and advocate for people with disabilities. Helen spent all of her adult life overcoming her suffering, pain, and how the world said she should respond. She showed others how to do the same. Didn't I say, that it is all how you view your circumstance? "For I have learned to be content whatever the circumstances" (Philippians 4:11b, NIV). I believe, with all certainty, that she didn't let this horrible experience mold her life into turmoil for very long. This might be difficult to understand or visualize for some, but you play the hand that you have been dealt to the best of your ability. All I can say is that we aren't victims of our circumstances, and we shouldn't be defined by them, no matter how cheated we feel. Children of God are never cheated.

Finally then, I can't help but view my own circumstances at this point. I sometimes feel cheated. I will not deny that the moments and days of quicksand are still around, though they are fewer than before, mostly because I choose not to entertain them. I don't like the way I feel, think, or act during those periods of time. I will concede that, occasionally, I listen to the world view as well as wonder, *Will that really work?* And I do find at times that it is a struggle to live for the moment, because I am still suffering even three years later, or to just start my day over. I admit that I am not without reading, watching, or looking for those hasty remedies to resolve this juncture in my life. Romans 12 reminds us to not look for these remedies in the world. "Do not conform to the pattern of this world, but be transformed by the renewing of your mind. Then you will be able to test and approve what God's will is—his good, pleasing and perfect will" (Romans 12:2, NIV).

Like most, I can entertain any idea from any source that seems plausible, even the ones that aren't supported through Christ. At the end of the day, these ways may seem easier or immediate, but they leave you searching for the truth and purpose. It is necessary for me to refer back to Jeremiah 29:11 (NIV): "'For I know the plans I have for you,' declares the LORD, 'plans to prosper you and not to harm you, plans to give you hope and a future.'" After reading this, how can I perceive my uncontrollable circumstances as harmful or as cheated in anyway? Isn't Christ telling us that in no way, shape, or form does His Father allow a condition to intervene that causes damage or impairment to our lives without there still being hope and purpose. Therefore, it is our job as Christians to devote our time and efforts to Christ whether in chaos or calm waters. When we search for Christ to satisfy us instead of the world, our needs are fulfilled with peace even though we may still suffer. Saint Paul writes: "May the God of hope fill you with all joy and peace as you trust in him, so that you may overflow with hope by the power of the Holy Spirit" (Romans 15:13, NIV).

The Bible is full of examples of where our Father has stepped in while his people were suffering and they were saved from harm. It has all been part of the plans he has for each and every one of us. Here is a brief lesson on some of God's plans to prosper and be satisfied. First of all, didn't God protect Daniel from the evils of his time? As it is written:

> "Daniel, servant of the living God, has your God, whom you serve continually, been able to rescue you from the lions?" Daniel answered, "May the king live forever! My God sent his angel and he shut the mouths of the lions. They have not hurt me, because I was found innocent in his sight. Nor have I ever done any wrong before you, Your Majesty." The king was over-joyed and gave orders to lift Daniel out of the den. And when Daniel was lifted from the den, no wound was found on him, because he had trusted in his God
>
> Daniel 6:20b-23 (NIV)

The king then punished the part of the "world" that tried to harm Daniel. He threw Daniel's accusers and their families to the lions, and they devoured them. In the same way, Paul confesses that God rescued him after he had been given the "sentence of death" while proclaiming the circumstances that were bestowed

upon him were so he would not rely on anything else, the world or himself, and rely only on the father, "who raises the dead." Thirdly, an angel of God was sent to free Peter from Herod's grasp in prison, and after Peter realized it wasn't a vision, he said in Acts 12:11 (NIV): "Now I know without a doubt that the Lord has sent his angel and rescued me from Herod's clutches and from everything the Jewish people were hoping would happen." Is Christ not the great "I Am"? Finally, weren't Shadrach, Meshach, and Abednego thrown into the blazing furnace by King Nebuchadnezzar for not falling down to worship the idol he had created? The king summoned them and inquired if they heard the direction he has given and they replied:

> King Nebuchadnezzar, we do not need to defend ourselves before you in this matter. If we are thrown into the blazing furnace, the God we serve is able to deliver us from it, and he will deliver us from Your Majesty's hand. But even if he does not, we want you to know, Your Majesty, that we will not serve your gods or worship the image of gold you have set up.
>
> Daniel 3:16b-18 (NIV)

They were thrown into the burning furnace which was seven times hotter than usual. It was so hot that the strongest soldiers that tied them up died from the flames. Now, to the king's amazement, when he looked into the blazing furnace, there were four men, not just three. But three were thrown in. In Daniel 3: 25 (NIV) the King said, "Look! I see four men walking around in the fire, unbound and unharmed, and the fourth looks like a son of the gods." King Nebuchadnezzar shouted at them to come out of the furnace. When they appeared before him he and the crowd were astonished. "They saw that the fire had not harmed their bodies, nor was a hair of their heads singed; their robes were not scorched, and there was no smell of fire on them" (Daniel 3:27b, NIV).

> Then Nebuchadnezzar said, "Praise be to the God of Shadrach, Meshach and Abednego, who has sent his angel and rescued his servants! They trusted in him and defied the king's command and were willing to give up their lives rather than serve or worship any god except their own God. Therefore I decree that the people of any nation or language who say anything against the God of Shadrach, Meshach and Abednego be cut into pieces and their houses be turned into piles of rubble, for no other god can save in this way."

After this, the King promoted Shadrach, Meshach and Abednego and believed in our God, the God that saved them, Daniel, Peter, Paul and us.

So I ask, is he not the Son of God and man that came so we would be saved like the ones before us? Is He not the son that is leading us to God for our salvation? The only way to God and eternal life is through Christ. Christ is like the guard to the door of salvation. He is the only one with the key to that entryway. "Do not be afraid. I am the First and the Last...and I hold the keys of death and Hades" (Revelation 1:17-18, NIV). Ultimately, that is the door I want unlocked for me at the end. I want my reward in heaven, at last. Isn't that the only way I will see my brother again? Isn't that why we are living bodies of Christ? If Christ is living in us, while we suffer through this evil, materialistic world, we will have peace of the promise. "Let the peace of Christ rule in your hearts, since as members of one body you were called to peace. And be thankful" (Colossians 3:15, NIV).

God had no plans to harm these men or to allow them to be harmed; He only gave them peace. He wanted them saved to fulfill his purpose in this world. He wanted to emphasize his power and greatness. He wanted to assert through these miracles what can happen if you just believe. He wanted to make clear, with every miracle, that Christ is the only way to Him and into the kingdom of heaven, not the ways or the people of the world. He wanted the world to see what happens if you trust Him and only Him. "Trust in the LORD with all your heart and lean not on your own understanding" (Proverbs 3:5—, NIV). It must have been quite difficult for Daniel, Shadrach, Meshach, Abednego, Paul, and Peter to trust that the Lord would deliver them. They had no hope for the fallen world to save them; their reliance and peace was with The Lord. This is no different in our world today. We don't get thrown into a literal den of a lions or blazing furnaces; nevertheless, we all have our own lion's den. We all have struggles in life that we seek to eliminate or at least find solace from. Mine is the death of my brother; yours could be similar, or a divorce, infertility, abuse, or unemployment. The list is endless, but peace and understanding is limitless.

With any struggle comes a search for resolution. The evil plays games with our head, and it is hard to resist what Satan says he has to offer. What he dangles in front of our noses. He says he can offer the world. That is lie; just ask Adam and Eve. It is written in Thessalonians 3:3 (NIV): " But the Lord is faithful, and he will strengthen you and protect you from the evil one." Believe that till the end. Satan and his universal evils have never solved a thing that us humans didn't regret. Now, what isn't tolerated is for us to search anywhere but the Word of God. The Word of God and the assurance in Christ is what will give us the perspective and salvation we yearn for. Second Corinthians 7:10 boasts: "Godly sorrow brings repentance that leads to salvation and leaves no regret, but worldly sorrow brings death" (NIV).

Sometimes, skepticism overwhelms us, but even at the last moment, God can rescue you. Never give up. Don't stay stuck in the quicksand. Use prayer as the rope to pull you out. Anger and depression will only enable you to remain lost and hopeless in your circumstance, whatever it is, and then we look for unconventional ways out. Believe, in all these things we are more than conquerors through Him who loved us. Saint Paul was pretty clear that nothing could divide us from Christ.

> "For I am convinced that neither death nor life, neither angels nor demons, neither the present nor the future, nor any powers, neither height nor depth, nor anything else in all creation, will

be able to separate us from the love of God that
is in Christ Jesus our Lord."

(Romans 8:38, NIV)

Who really is cheated? Was Helen cheated when
she lost her hearing and sight? Was Daniel cheated
when he was throne into the den of lions? Am I cheated
because my brother isn't here? The world may say I've
been double-crossed; the world may try to persuade me
of this, yet most days I feel blessed that he has been
victorious in death. I received the short end of the stick
since I still await my heavenly home. Though I forge
ahead as it is written in Philippians 3:14 (NIV): "I press
on toward the goal to win the prize for which God
has called me heavenward in Christ Jesus." Philippians
continues on to remind us that heaven is where our cit-
izenship lies, not this God-made earthly sphere, and we
should be on the edge of our seat with anticipation for
the Savior to arrive: the one and only Lord Jesus Christ.
"Look, I am coming soon! My reward is with me, and
I will give to each person according to what they have
done" (Revelation 22:12, NIV). Therefore, I sure don't
want to be cheated from my reward as a result of something I did or didn't do on earth. The answer is that I
am not cheated because Josh is gone, I have discovered
that I am the only one that can cheat myself from being
reunited with him. I know, even at my young age, that
God has given me an abundance of time to make an
impact for Him on this world. I hope, with all things
considered, I haven't let the world and its perspectives,

deceptions, and lies influence me too much. I pray that I continue to follow the Spirit of truth.

> Because the one who is in you is greater than the one who is in the world. They are from the world and therefore speak from the viewpoint of the world, and the world listens to them. We are from God, and whoever knows God listens to us; but whoever is not from God does not listen to us. This is how we recognize the Spirit of truth and the spirit of falsehood.
>
> 1 John 4:4-6 (NIV)

"For the kingdom of God is not a matter of talk but of power."
(1 Corinthians 4:20, NIV)

The loss of Josh has taught me one very important lesson, probably the greatest lesson I will ever learn. This lesson is that I don't want to be hanging around wondering if I am a sheep or a goat when those trumpets sound. It is written in Matthew that Christ will return in his entire splendor and that "All the nations will be gathered before him, and he will separate the people one from another as a shepherd separates the sheep from the goats" (Matthew 25:32). If the sheep are ushered to Christ's side, where do you think the goats are being escorted? I believe that there truly is a final destination. Christ, without a doubt, is the Son of God and man, and he absolutely died on the cross for *our* sins, rose again, and now sits at the right hand of God, waiting for the finale. It is written:

> Do not let your hearts be troubled. You believe in God; believe also in me. My Father's house has many rooms; if that were not so, would I have told you that I am going there to prepare a place for you? And if I go and prepare a place for you, I will come back and take you to be with me that you also may be where I am.
>
> John 14:1-3 (NIV).

I would like to say it one more time, if you have faith and believe, then you know this promise from the Son is true. In the same respect then, you know the answer to the questions. Where do the goats go? The only destination for those goats is eternity with the fallen angel, the fallen angel that was cast down from the heavens as written in Luke 10:18(NIV): "I saw Satan fall like lightning from heaven." If you arc wondering, the same thing is true for those that have gone before us; they have been accompanied to heaven (sheep) or banished to hell (goats). This is why I am certain about that. Daniel explains, "Multitudes who sleep in the dust of the earth will awake: some to everlasting life, others to shame and everlasting contempt" (Daniel 12:2 NIV). Also, in Luke 16, where the rich man called to father Abraham after being sent to an eternal life of torment;

> "The time came when the beggar died and the angels carried him to Abraham's side. The rich man also died and was buried, in Hades, where he was in torment, he looked up and saw Abraham far away, with Lazarus by his side."
>
> (Luke 16:20-23 NIV)

The rich man cried out for relief from this torment in the next verses: "So he called to him, 'Father Abraham, have pity on me and send Lazarus to dip the tip of his finger in water and cool my tongue, because I am in agony in this fire.'" Abraham sums it up by saying he had a chance while on earth and that it is too late for him. Once the rich man realized this was his punishment for eternity, he then begged that Lazarus would be sent back to appear to his brothers so that they would believe and be saved. Still, Abraham denied the request, telling him that his brothers should trust in the prophets and Moses, and if not, they will be herded with the goats. You see, there is no second chance after this life, you make your choices while here, either run the race while jumping the hurdles or trip on a shoelace and stay down. The pain of not getting back up is nothing compared to the torment ahead.

It is safe to assume that the torment of hell must be just that: torturous. Why else would the rich man want to come back? "And the devil, who deceived them, was thrown into the lake of burning sulfur, where the beast and the false prophet had been thrown. They will be tormented day and night forever and ever" (Revelation 20:10b, NIV). Another verse describes the persecution in more depth: 2 Thessalonians 1:9: "They will suffer the punishment of eternal destruction, away from the presence of the Lord and from the glory of his might." There is no greater suffering than the suffering one will endure when separated from the love of Christ. Look what this Man has done for us. Because He paid our debt with each pound of the hammer and every drip of blood, we don't bear the true depths of hell on earth. This is our only chance to accept him as the one and only true son of God that was born to man who suffered and was buried, died and then rose from the dead on the third day, who is now living with the Father, and is coming again. For those that don't, they will be judged for every wrong doing and will be sentenced to death, once more.

> And I saw the dead, great and small, standing before the throne, and books were opened. Another book was opened, which is the book of life. The dead were judged according to what they had done as recorded in the books…and each person was judged according to what they had done. Then death and Hades were thrown into the lake of fire. The lake of fire is the second death. Anyone whose name was not found written in the book of life was thrown into the lake of fire.

Revelation 10:12-15(NIV)

As if dying once wasn't bad enough; the goats will die again.

That fiery description is horrifying. Life is much simpler when living for our souls and not our lives. Living for our souls requires little work. How much work does it require to just be faithful, pray, and follow and believe God's Word? This takes much less time and energy than satisfying every sinful, earthly desire it takes to keep up with the Joneses. The Joneses lack the time to satisfy their soul because they are too busy indulging in the world to reflect on the spirit. That is time wasted when there is money to be made and earthly lives to be lived. The earthly self can see the riches of this earth given by man and can easily ignore the ones given by God. They will answer for every disobedience, and those of us living through the eyes of righteousness will receive the promise. First Peter 1:8-9 (NIV):

> "Though you have not seen him, you love him; and even though you do not see him now, you

believe in him and are filled with an inexpress-
ible and glorious joy, for you are receiving the
end result of your faith, the salvation of your
souls."

My brother's soul is exactly where my parents hoped
it would be: with the Lord. He understood the kingdom
of God wasn't just show. He loved God and had faith in
Him without seeing. He believed the truth is the Word
and that he also awaits the homecoming of all the souls,
including our families and mine, whenever God decides
to sound the trumpets. "Multitudes who sleep in the dust
of the earth will awake: some to everlasting life, others to
shame and everlasting contempt" (Daniel 12:2, NIV).

No one but the Father himself knows when the
trumpets will sound. No one but the Father himself
knows when the dead will be raised and that book of
life will be opened, but Christ does say in Revelation:
"Behold, I am coming soon! Blessed is he who keeps
the words of the prophecy in this book" (Revelation
22:7, NIV). My grandfather told us years ago that he
would never hear the trumpets, but he was sure that
we, his grandchildren, would. Now that I am older, I
think Christ's reentry will be in my children's generation and not mine, unlike what my grandpa thought. It
is a guessing game, and all that matters is that, whenever that time comes, the people of this world are ready,
because there may not be a tomorrow, and one day
there won't be. On that day, people will be wishing they
had heeded the warnings. The words of the prophecy
give us clues to the end:

> But mark this: There will be terrible times in
> the last days. People will be lovers of them-
> selves, lovers of money, boastful, proud, abusive,
> disobedient to their parents, ungrateful, unholy,
> without love, unforgiving, slanderous, with-
> out self-control, brutal, not lovers of the good,
> treacherous, rash, conceited, lovers of pleasure
> rather than lovers of God—having a form of
> godliness but denying its power. Have nothing
> to do with such people.

1 Timothy 3:1-5 (NIV)

Wow, that is the world we live in today. The book of Revelation, written by the apostle John from a dream, tells of the ceasing of life on earth and of the launching of the new spiritual life. The book of Matthew warns of signs such as false prophets, famine, wars, and rumors of wars, earthquakes, pestilence, and increased sin. These things have been happening for years. War and famine, somewhere in the world, has never been at a standstill. Sin has steadily increased since the apple episode.

These signs could leave you guessing, so I just choose to have faith that the day will come to pass, sooner or later. It will happen when God says so, no one else. False prophets have a tendency to take a little here and there of the Bible and profess they have the answer to the end. God is the one and only one that knows when the world will end. He most certainly isn't announcing that on Wikipedia, or making a video that goes viral. Josh's death has illustrated to me that I am Jesus little lamb, baptized through Christ and that my little lamb name can be found under my parents in the book of life. But those who names are not written: "The inhabitants of the earth whose names have not been written in the book of life from the creation of the world will be astonished when they see the beast" (Revelation 17:8, NIV). They will be like the rich man: begging.

I can understand how people would scoff at the notion that this all came to John in a vision from an angel. If John made this entire vision up, then one may think that he was a better writer than Stephen King. The book of Revelation can bring forth some frightening visualizations, but there is a mountain of beauty that he describes as well. Apostle John makes it clear that he is not the author of Revelation, just the vessel. He tells us that Christ himself is the author. "The revelation from Jesus Christ, which God gave him to show his servants what must soon take place. He made it known by sending his angel to his servant John, who testifies to everything he saw—that is, the word of God and the testimony of Jesus Christ" (Revelation 1:1-2, NIV). We shouldn't be surprised that He chose a human to be the vessel. He has done that many times over in the Bible. John continues on by telling us that Christ is coming soon and those that believe will reap the benefits. "Blessed is the one who reads aloud the words of this prophecy, and blessed are those who hear it and take to heart what is written in it, because the time is near" (Revelation 1:3, NIV). John continues by saying if you don't have faith that the word is the truth, then heaven isn't the place for you. And really, what a simple concept: just have faith and believe in the words of the prophecy.

I wonder if our Father ever sits up there on his throne, scratching his head in awe of this world, in awe because He doesn't ask too much. Nevertheless, we make it difficult. In awe that the world he created in seven days has, many times, turned it's back on Him. In awe that the some of the sheep He loves will never reap the benefits to reach the streets of gold. I often conjure up images of Josh walking around on these streets, amazed at the beauty of it all. I don't know, but I believe it would be too difficult to take it all in in just a short time. "The great street of the city was of gold, as pure as transparent glass" (Revelation 21:21b, NIV). Can anyone truly grasp the full splendor of the city? The book of Revelation is very precise about the picturesque scenery in heaven: walls of jasper and precious stones everywhere, gates made of pearl and the glory of God shining through, giving light. Wow, what a scenic view. I have seen some amazing sites, personally and through other images in my life, but I don't believe that any of them can compare to the scenes created by reading these verses. As I thumb through the visuals in my mind, no real image I have can begin to do it justice; I guess I will just have to wait for my turn.

Revelation does give a little insight into heaven, like the visual description on the city. The other details that Christ allows us to know are minute, but still some observations are better than none. John explains that the entire world will be washed away from us. We will not experience the things of the world in heaven; after all, this is where righteousness dwells. From his description, it is a fair bet that we will, more than likely, not remember the world after our name is called. "Nothing impure will ever enter it, nor will anyone who does what is shameful or deceitful, but only those whose names are written in the Lamb's book of life" (Revelation 21:27, NIV).

Finally, who has the power to forgive? Who has granted us the ability to repent? That is our Father, and when I take communion, I ask for forgiveness for my sins. I am satisfied that Josh on that Sunday did the same, even though he didn't realize that his time was near. "Repent, for the kingdom of heaven has come near" (Matthew 4:17, NIV). The kingdom was much closer for him that day than he knew. It is written that God will not come with all his glory until everything is accomplished; that could be today or one hundred years from now. Whether today, tomorrow, or one hundred years from now, I know that the prophecy is true and is being fulfilled. I know that I am planting a seed for my children and for generations to come. I know that Josh's death was part of His beautiful plan, and I know that, one day, we will walk the streets of gold together, but not everyone will. Those that refuse to believe the truth will not enjoy what is ahead of them. "Not everyone who says to me, 'Lord, Lord,' will enter the kingdom of heaven, but only the one who does the will of my Father who is in heaven" (Matthew 7:21, NIV).

"I thank my God every time I remember you." (Philippians 1:3, NIV)

"What an agonizing day it was three years ago. It was the last day we saw the light in your eyes. It was the last day our family was together and whole. We are forever changed with your passing but you are basking in the everlasting light of salvation. When the chair is pulled out for me it will be the one next to you. We will be together again one day, as a whole family. Oh, the things you have missed that I wish I could tell you about. I love you with all my heart and soul, and when I remember you, I smile. Satan is a liar; he was correct that things are different, but he was wrong when he said we would be ruined. Our family is stronger than ever standing firm on the rock of our salvation." I wrote this to my brother three years after he died.

This week is always the hardest of the year for us. I think we battle with this week for different reasons: it is Christmas week and we were in the hospital for close to three days with him before Christmas, and services were directly after Christmas. There are many memories of that week, and when they are the last memories you have, you hold on for the ride as you relive them. Part of me also believes that it is almost a self-fulfilling prophecy, so to speak, and we just convince ourselves we have to jump feet first into the quicksand during this time, but I have a constant phrase in my head, especially during this season: "Satan is a liar."

Pastor Ryan stated in the funeral sermon: "Satan is a liar." If you believe Satan is a liar, then you believe me when I tell you Christmas will never change. Satan telling me Christmas is forever changed is just another lie. I remind myself of this often. Josh's death doesn't change the way I view Christmas. Christmas remains the same and I can remember Josh without believing the lies. I can remember without remaining in bed in the fetal position. I can hold on to the ride of memories, and when I get off, turn around and smile. Just because Christmas reminds me of a lousy moment in time doesn't mean that it correlates at all with Christmas. These two occasions just happen to fall in the same time period every year. See the point I am driving home? I can remember the good, bad, and ugly without it overshadowing the spirit of Christmas. Jesus is the reason we live on earth and the reason we will live in heaven. The idea of Christmas has never changed; it has remained constant for thousands of years. We are the ones that change our traditions and ideas of what Christmas is about. We are the ones that made the birth of Christ about Santa, trees, and gifts. The two-horned creature perpetuates these man-made traditions every year in hopes that we forget the true meaning of Christmas. For us, that fatal week three years ago marked our first Christmas without him. Our traditions changed dramatically that week, but we never lost sight of the meaning. Even though he isn't physically with us, we are reminded of him at every turn.

This prime example of Satan's lies is "Christmas will never be the same." Remember, he is a liar. Christmas will never change; only our perception will change if we let it. This year our traditions changed when my parents invited Betsy's new husband, Wes, to our family Christmas, and they obliged. This year we started new traditions. It was important to include the only father figure my niece will know, and as far as we are concerned, that makes him family. The three of them spent part of their Christmas day with us, and there were more smiles than tears for the first time in a long time. There was a sense of peace around the dinner table that included Betsy and her new husband, a sense of joy and happiness that had been missing for years. It is no picnic to suffer, and the more your mind is swamped with memories and thoughts, the harder it seems to be to move in any direction. With Christ, you can climb your Mount Everest. You see, the pain of grief hasn't been allowed to infiltrate our lives forever because we believe. If your life is lead through Christ, grief is just a passing snowstorm on the mount. Trust me, there is no hard and fast rule about when you will recognize the clearing sky in the rough terrain, but you will. Remember this, nowhere in the rules of grieving does it say I have to remain rooted or immobilized. One should never stop moving through the process of grief. Make new traditions while remembering the old ones. Write your memories down in a journal, talk about them as much as you can, and keep praying.

Memories are wonderful things, but they can be quite painful. Memories are some of the moments that you feel completely disabled. A memory is most always accompanied by a feeling and when the memory is about my brother, then I feel agony again, especially when there is a group of us joined together remembering him. Josh's friends organize a poker/memorial run every year. It is overwhelming to know that we aren't the only ones that remember or miss him terribly. We aren't the only ones changed by his life and death. This is probably when the sadness is the worst: when there are others around sharing in the sadness. It can be almost debilitating, even today. The Bible says in these times we should continue to be faithful and do the right thing, which is in accordance to our Father's will. "So then, those who suffer according to God's will should commit themselves to their faithful Creator and continue to do good" (1 Peter 4:19, NIV). Our Father says, even when we don't feel like we can maneuver another hurdle, and we are weak, hold onto his grace and mercy, follow His words and will, and He will lead us home. "My grace is sufficient for you, for my power is made perfect in weakness" (2 Corinthians 12:9, NIV). This is cause for celebration, smile.

If the Father's power is made perfect in our vulnerability, then it shouldn't be an issue to be smiling, but how or why would you smile in the face of vulnerability? This is why. We are smiling and feeling joy because of His splendid power by which his plan is being fulfilled. When I remember, it isn't just the old memories of Josh and his life, it is the new memories of Josh's eternal life and how ours have changed. I can't help but think about him in a newfound light, the light of everlasting peace. That thought alone can leave a smile on my face for days. Someday I too will be dancing in that light as I am absolutely certain that my name is written in that book: "but rejoice that your names are written in heaven" (Luke 10:20, NIV). This delights me as I type because I too will have a new body in Christ. "For we know that if the earthly tent we live in is destroyed, we have a building from God, an eternal house in heaven, not built by human hands" (2 Corinthians 5:1, NIV). We will not have to hold onto all the pains, concerns, burdens, and griefs we carry now.

Christ says, in John 16, that we will suffer but smile, knowing that He himself carried our burden and death sentence. "I have said these things to you, that in me you may have peace. In the world you will have tribulation. But take heart; I have overcome the world" (John 16:33, NIV). Additionally, it is also said in Revelation 21:4 (NIV): "He will wipe every tear from their eyes. There will be no more death or mourning or crying or pain, for the old order of things has passed away." Again I ask, why smile? Smile because we don't have the sentence of death anymore. Smile because Christ took the punishment for us so that not only would He be raised and live again, but so that we may live also. Smile because he is alive and we are promised eternal salvation. "Whoever believes in the Son has eternal life, but whoever rejects the Son will not see life, for God's wrath remains on them" (John 3:36, NIV). I am convinced that I have experienced enough sufferings in this world; I most definitely don't want the wrath to be upon me in the next.

Every time I remember my brother, I thank God. I thank Him for that last period of time we had together at a little boy's birthday party. God could have allowed this to happen any other way, but he chose to guide them to church, communion, Bible class, a family party, and then the unthinkable. Josh spent his final days and hours with the most important people in his life. I like to think that he has memories of us, but that would mean I have to believe that he remembers earthly things that, I know, in heaven are not allowed. I found this concept difficult for many months: that he had no remembrance his life on earth, of our family, or me. Moreover, it was difficult to swallow that we wouldn't be the traditional family in heaven that we were here on earth. In heaven we are all family and we recognize everyone, not just our loved ones. Scripture displays it several different times in the Bible. In the transfiguration, the disciples recognized Moses and Elijah even though they weren't told who they were. Moses had lived 1500 years before Peter, James, and John yet they recognized him. Elijah went to heaven in his body, having never died. Moses and his body had not yet been resurrected. Both men were recognizable to the apostles.

It is tough to accept that we don't live in one little home as a family unit, we all live as a family, praising and worshiping one true God. Life everlasting isn't about our own little world; it is about God. One of the biggest lessons I have learned from Pastor Helmkamp is "It won't matter in Heaven." What makes me smile here, what causes me pain, what I did for a living, or who will remember me won't even be a thought. Once

you can get past that earthly thinking and start thinking heavenly, the easier it is to smile. One example is
when I take communion; it feels just as though I can
just reach out and slide the veil to get a glimpse of what
is going on on the other side. As I kneel at the communion rail to partake of Christ's body and blood while
those glorious saints communion with us, it as if I can
peek behind that Oz-like curtain and see him partak-
ing in the body and blood with me as a family, as we did
for so many years. When I started thinking heavenly
and not earthly, the pieces of the puzzle began to fit.
Life as I knew it made some sense, and then I gained
the realization that heaven really isn't that far away, it's
just on the other side. When I recognize God's handiwork in everything, it seems elementary. And I smile.

Josh lives there with the Lord, awaiting Christ's
return and rooting us on as we run the race. Do I desire
him to be here with us, as a family, raising his daughter?
Yes. Although, if God gave me a choice to bring him
back or let him stay, I would request that he stay. There
is nothing important enough in this world to come
back to the pain, suffering, and discomfort of a fallen
world. He is where the people of this world should be
aching to be one day. Josh's death, not his life, will help
lead others to the cross and eternal life. Josh's death
brought the whispering words of God to my heart and
soul, and hence, this manuscript was written. It may be
rough around the edges, but so am I. Once I internalized that I was the vessel for writing this, I was truly
humbled. The realization that, because of Josh's death,
this was written and people will be brought closer to

Christ, which in itself is in an amazing experience, is also humbling. Because I choose to look through with heavenly glasses, I can see part of the plan unfolding, though I will never see the whole design. I have a glimpse of it and I know now that, Josh's death wasn't in vain. If he only knew his death would save lives.

Josh's life was changed because he no longer has this sinful garb wrapped around him. "For we know that if the earthly tent we live in is destroyed, we have a building from God, an eternal house in heaven, not built by human hands" (2 Corinthians 5:1-2, NIV). I still wear the sinful clothing, though I have forever been changed and have learned what real longing is about. "Meanwhile we groan, longing to be clothed instead with our heavenly dwelling" (2 Corinthians 5:2, NIV). Our family has not only adapted, but we have evolved throughout this process. Since his perishable clothing has been taken off, our family has truly gotten a taste of what this journey is all about. It is written in Matthew 24:35-36 (NIV): "Heaven and earth will pass away, but my words will never pass away But about that day or hour no one knows, not even the angels in heaven, nor the Son, but only the Father." This passage through life is about living for the beginning, not the end.

This jaunt we are all on is only a short run, and I've discovered if I don't have the proper running shoes on, my soul wears down quickly and is left on the side of the road. I have now internalized this fact. Each one of us is on our trek, not really knowing if or when the trail will end, but having knowledge when the gravel road ceases on earth, the green light says go in heaven.

I smile when I see his face and hear his laugh. I have faith that we will meet again. I feel blessed when God whispers to my soul: "Josh loves you." Romans 6:23 (NIV) says it best: "For the wages of sin is death, but the gift of God is eternal life in Christ Jesus our Lord." That, my dear friends, should make you smile.